By Emily Mahoney

Portions of this book originally appeared in *Overweight America* by Meryl Loonin.

Published in 2018 by
Lucent Press, an Imprint of Greenhaven Publishing, LLC
353 3rd Avenue
Suite 255
New York, NY 10010

Designer: Andrea Davison-Bartolotta
Editor: Jennifer Lombardo

Cataloging-in-Publication Data

Names: Mahoney, Emily.
Title: Obesity: an American epidemic / Emily Mahoney.
Description: New York : Lucent Press, 2018. | Series: Hot topics | Includes index.
Identifiers: ISBN 9781534561472 (library bound) | ISBN 9781534561489 (ebook)
Subjects: LCSH: Obesity–Juvenile literature.
Classification: LCC RC628.M34 2018 | DDC 616.3'98–dc23

Printed in the United States of America

CPSIA compliance information: Batch #BS17KL: For further information contact Greenhaven Publishing LLC, New York, New York at 1-844-317-7404.

Please visit our website, www.greenhavenpublishing.com. For a free color catalog of all our high-quality books, call toll free 1-844-317-7404 or fax 1-844-317-7405.

CONTENTS

Adolescence is a time when many people begin to take notice of the world around them. News channels, blogs, and talk radio shows are constantly promoting one view or another; very few are unbiased. Young people also hear conflicting information from parents, friends, teachers, and acquaintances. Often, they will hear only one side of an issue or be given flawed information. People who are trying to support a particular viewpoint may cite inaccurate facts and statistics on their blogs, and news programs present many conflicting views of important issues in our society. In a world where it seems everyone has a platform to share their thoughts, it can be difficult to find unbiased, accurate information about important issues.

It is not only facts that are important. In blog posts, in comments on online videos, and on talk shows, people will share opinions that are not necessarily true or false, but can still have a strong impact. For example, many young people struggle with their body image. Seeing or hearing negative comments about particular body types online can have a huge effect on the way someone views himself or herself and may lead to depression and anxiety. Although it is important not to keep information hidden from young people under the guise of protecting them, it is equally important to offer encouragement on issues that affect their mental health.

The titles in the Hot Topics series provide readers with different viewpoints on important issues in today's society. Many of these issues, such as teen pregnancy and Internet safety, are of immediate concern to young people. This series aims to give readers factual context on these crucial topics in a way that lets them form their own opinions. The facts presented throughout also serve to empower readers to help themselves or support people they know who are struggling with many of the challenges adolescents face today. Although negative viewpoints are not ignored or downplayed, this series allows young people to see that the challenges they face are not insurmountable. Eating disorders can be overcome, the Internet can be navigated safely, and pregnant teens do not have to feel hopeless.

Quotes encompassing all viewpoints are presented and cited so readers can trace them back to their original source, verifying for themselves whether the information comes from a reputable place. Additional books and websites are listed, giving readers a starting point from which to continue their own research. Chapter questions encourage discussion, allowing young people to hear and understand their classmates' points of view as they further solidify their own. Full-color photographs and enlightening charts provide a deeper understanding of the topics at hand. All of these features augment the informative text, helping young people understand the world they live in and formulate their own opinions concerning the best way they can improve it.

A Problem on the Rise

Weight is an increasing problem in the United States; nearly three-quarters of adults over the age of 20 are overweight or obese (severely overweight), and nearly half of all children between the ages of 2 and 19 are obese. Health experts warn that the problem has become an epidemic.

There are many complex reasons for this weight epidemic. Growing portion sizes; the wide availability of cheap, unhealthy food; a move toward a more sedentary society (where people sit for long periods of time and get little exercise); a desire for quick fixes rather than a willingness to make lifestyle changes; and inaccurate information about how best to lose weight have all contributed in one way or another to this problem.

Doctors and nutritionists have been sounding the alarm about the dangers of Americans' unhealthy diets and lack of exercise for decades, but the public has reacted with indifference and inaction. Many Americans believe that those who are obese are personally responsible for lacking the discipline and willpower to get in shape. The country's huge fast food, snack-food, and soda industries have encouraged this belief. They have pushed hard to persuade elected officials and the public that weight gain should remain a matter of private rather than public concern. As a result, the issue has often remained low on the national agenda.

Only as weight gain and obesity have spread to affect Americans of all ages and income levels, and especially as more children and teens have been affected by it, has the problem become too widespread to ignore. In recent years, media coverage of the issue has exploded. It has become difficult to pick up a newspaper or turn on a TV news or talk show without hearing about an obesity crisis. Doctors, nutritionists, and politicians all speak out publicly on the issue of weight. Pharmaceutical companies devote tremendous resources and energy to the search for

Many people do not get enough exercise and eat unhealthy, processed food, leading to weight gain.

weight-loss drugs and treatments.

However, many health experts believe that the key to the nation's obesity problem lies in the unhealthy—some even say toxic—environment in which Americans live, work, and spend their leisure time. It is an environment in which super-size portions are the norm and grocery stores stock a dizzying variety of snack foods, frozen desserts, and sugary cereals. Encouragements to eat high-calorie foods are everywhere. U.S. children are exposed to junk food commercials every time they tune in to their favorite TV programs. People who live in poverty often find that a small amount of healthy food and a large amount of unhealthy food cost the same amount, generally leading them to choose the option that will give them the most food for the lowest cost.

Life in America has also become increasingly sedentary, and many Americans spend more time sitting at a desk than moving around. Cities sprawl across vast distances, forcing people to spend hours in their cars or on the bus. Leisure time activities frequently involve sitting still in front of a television, computer, phone, or movie screen.

How Much of a Threat Is It?

Despite these trends, some social critics downplay the threat that obesity poses to the nation. They argue that Americans have simply become victims of their own prosperity. Obesity and weight gain, they say, are problems that affect nations of the world in which food is plentiful and affordable. Radley Balko, an advocate for less government interference in people's lives, wrote, "Not only has our remarkable economy managed to feed all of its citizens, our chief worry right now seems to be that our poor and middle class have too much to eat. That's a remarkable achievement."[1]

Nutritionists and health experts counter that obesity is linked to serious and life-threatening illnesses and disabilities that carry enormous economic and public health costs.

Children are increasingly forming poor eating habits, which has contributed to a rise in obesity among all ages.

Low-income Americans often bear a disproportionate share of the health burden. Although they suffer less frequently from the desperate hunger and malnutrition that plague people in the poorest nations of the world, they often lack access to nutritious foods, such as fruits and vegetables, that promote good health and protect against disease. Francine R. Kaufman, a doctor who has treated many children with obesity-related diseases, said, "Listening to my young patients talk about their lives, I become angry at a society that doesn't seem to care, at an economic structure that makes it cheaper to eat fries than fruit, and at the food industry and the mass media luring children to consume what should not be consumed."[2]

Health advocates such as Kaufman argue that Americans can no longer afford not to worry about the nation's growing obesity problem or to treat extreme weight gain as solely a matter of personal responsibility. They insist that public and private institutions must play an active role in helping to reverse unhealthy diet and lifestyle trends that have taken hold over the past several decades. The goal, these advocates say, is to stop solely placing blame on the individuals in American society who become overweight or obese and instead to work to bring about broader, more lasting changes in an environment that promotes weight gain and makes unhealthy eating and inactivity accepted ways of life.

CHAPTER 1

Americans' Weight and Health

Turn on the news or radio, look at the many magazines at the grocery store, or view an Internet ad for weight loss: The message is everywhere that Americans are gaining weight at an alarming pace. Doctors, politicians, scientists, and dietitians are sounding the alarm that being overweight or obese can lead to health risks such as diabetes and heart disease. They also warn that obesity is costing the nation billions of dollars in medical care and hospital visits. Richard H. Carmona, the U.S. Surgeon General from 2002 to 2006 and one of the nation's most prominent public health officials, issued a call to action, telling the public that obesity is "every bit as threatening to us as is the terrorist threat we face today. It is the threat from within."[3]

Although obesity and weight gain are quickly becoming worldwide trends, the United States leads the way in terms of widespread obesity. In fact, extreme weight gain has replaced malnutrition as the number one food problem in many parts of the world. In America, bigger is often thought of as better, and Americans' waistlines are expanding along with the size of their burgers and soft drinks.

With breaking stories about diet and weight in the news almost daily, doctors and scientists are working to understand the threat that obesity poses to the nation. They attempt to track weight gain in the population, learn who is most affected by rising rates of obesity, and evaluate the real impact obesity has on Americans' long-term health and well-being.

How Is Obesity Determined?

The measure that most medical professionals use to determine if a person is overweight or obese is a ratio of weight and height called the body mass index (BMI). BMI is calculated by dividing a person's weight in pounds by his or her height in inches squared, then multiplied by 703. This converts to weight in kilograms divided by height in meters squared. BMI is a quick and easy way to calculate how much body fat individuals carry relative to their height and whether they fall in a healthy weight range or one that puts them at high risk for developing weight-related illness. It can be obtained without elaborate equipment or training. Only an accurate scale and height-measuring rod are needed. This makes it a practical means for scientists around the world to track and compare weight gain among different populations.

The U.S. government's Centers for Disease Control and Prevention (CDC) has established a normal range for BMI for adults of any height or shape. A BMI is considered normal if it falls between 18.5 and 24.5. This means that for a woman of average height—5 feet 4 inches tall (163 cm)—a normal BMI translates to a weight of between 108 and 144 pounds (49 and 65 kg). For a man of average height—5 feet 9 inches tall (175 cm)—the normal range falls between 125 and 168 pounds (57 and 76 kg). If an adult's BMI is between 25 and 29.9, the CDC guidelines place him or her in the overweight category. Any number higher than 30 is considered obese.

In recent years, health officials have promoted BMI as a way for people to assess their own weight status and set achievable weight-loss goals. Dozens of websites have sprung up that allow users to plug in their height and weight and calculate their own BMIs. However, some people object to the reliance on BMI to measure and compare weight gain. They argue that using such limited information to determine a person's physical condition and health risks means that people who are relatively healthy may be mislabeled as overweight or obese. The problem, they say, is that BMI makes no distinction between body fat and lean body mass, or muscle. It does not take into account whether a person exercises regularly and where his or her fat is located on the body, yet all of these can have a major impact on overall health.

Critics of BMI, including groups representing food and restaurant companies, often point out that fit and muscular celebrities and athletes such as football star Tony Romo, actor and former California governor Arnold Schwarzenegger, movie stars Tom Cruise and Dwayne "The Rock" Johnson, and others are all considered either overweight or obese based solely on their BMIs. Medical experts agree that BMI has flaws, but they say it is still the easiest and least expensive tool they have to monitor patients' weight and risk of disease. BMI is most useful in tracking the weight of large groups of people, rather than individuals. It allows researchers to track rates of obesity in a given population—for example, Americans—over a period of time. Doctors may calculate the BMI of individual patients, but they can then examine the patient more closely to see whether the number is an accurate indicator of that person's health.

BMI is also used to assess children's weight. However, it is interpreted differently, because children grow and develop in

BMI is a subjective measure. Athletes who have high amounts of muscle, such as quarterback Tony Romo, are often considered overweight by BMI measures.

very different ways as they mature. A child's BMI is calculated with the formula used for adults, but there are no set ranges to indicate that he or she is underweight or overweight. Instead, children's BMIs are compared on growth charts with those of other children of the same age and gender. For example, if a 10-year-old girl has a BMI that falls in the 60th percentile of the growth chart, then her BMI is higher than 60 percent of girls her own age. Only when a child's BMI is at or above the 85th percentile of the growth chart for his or her height, gender, and age is that child considered overweight. Those who are considered obese fall above the 95th percentile.

Diet and Weight Trends

Using BMI as a measure, there is no question that a greater percentage of Americans are overweight than they were 50, 20, or even 10 years ago. In fact, according to a study conducted between 2013 and 2014, more than 70 percent of American adults ages 20 and over are overweight or obese. The number stands around 20 percent for adolescents ages 12 to 19, and at 17 percent for children ages 6 to 11. Most alarming is that 8 percent of adults have a BMI greater than or equal to 40, which means they are extremely obese. Weight gain and obesity among Americans are growing so fast that health surveys can hardly keep pace. Since the late 1970s, the percentage of obese adults has doubled—from 15 to 37 percent. Eric Schlosser, author of the book *Fast Food Nation*, wrote, "No other nation in history has gotten so fat so fast."[4]

Obesity affects people in all segments of the U.S. population, in every state across the nation, and among both sexes, regardless of age, race, or ethnic background. Increasingly, it affects people of all income and educational levels.

Groups Most Vulnerable to Weight Gain

Despite the evidence that obesity is growing among wealthy Americans, health experts have known for decades that those who are most vulnerable to extreme weight gain and obesity are often poor. Economic and lifestyle factors play a role in ensuring that obesity and poverty go hand in hand. Healthy foods are typically more expensive than unhealthy foods and, therefore, more difficult for low-income people to afford. It is cheaper, for example, to buy a bag of chips than a pound of apples. There are also fewer places to purchase healthy foods in most poor neighborhoods. Many supermarket chains are reluctant to open stores in communities with high crime rates or visible signs of poverty, such as homelessness. Instead, these neighborhoods often have an abundance of fast food chains and small markets that sell high-calorie packaged foods. Residents of these neighborhoods not only have few healthy food options, they may also lack access to parks, playgrounds, bike paths, and other areas where they can safely walk and exercise. They are most likely not able to afford to join a gym or pay for exercise classes either, which some people credit with helping them lose weight.

Health experts say the large concentration of racial minorities and immigrant groups in many poor communities helps explain why blacks, Latinx, and Native Americans have extremely high rates of excess weight and obesity. "Obesity rates are higher among Blacks (48.4 percent) and Latinos (42.6 percent) than among Whites (36.4 percent) and Asian Americans (12.6 percent),"[5] according to the 2013–2014 National Health and Nutrition Examination Survey. Native Americans were not included in the study, but their rates of obesity are comparable to those of blacks and Latinx. Severe obesity is far more common among these racial groups than in the general population. Women are also more likely to be affected than men, although not enough research has been done yet to determine why this is. In every region of the country, those who are the most likely to be severely obese and to suffer the accompanying physical illness and reduced quality of life are poor women of color.

Obesity in Children and Teens

Unhealthy diets and lifestyles are at the root of the obesity problem not only for poor and minority Americans, but also for children of all income levels in the United States. The current generation of children in the United States is less fit and more prone to obesity than any other generation in history. Across the United States, childhood obesity rates have stayed at around 17 percent for more than 14 years. The obesity rate among 2- to 5-year-olds has declined. However, the rate for 6- to 11-year-olds has remained stable, and the rate increased for 12- to 19-year-olds.

The problem has become so widespread that the U.S. military has considered easing its weight standards for new teenage and young adult recruits. Many Americans of recruiting age weigh too much to be eligible to serve in the U.S. military.

Obesity is a growing problem among children. Children who are overweight are much more likely to suffer from a variety of health issues.

Surveys show that the children and teenagers most affected by obesity mirror those of the adult population. Children of black, Latinx, and Native American descent are the most susceptible to extreme weight gain. For example, "among preschoolers (ages 2 to 5), Latinos (7.6 percent) and Blacks (8.6 percent) are almost twice as likely to be extremely obese as Whites (4.4 percent)."[6] In some heavily minority school districts, it is not unusual for as many as half of the students in a classroom to be overweight. The problem was most pronounced in school districts with mainly Latinx and black students, many of whom also come from low-income families.

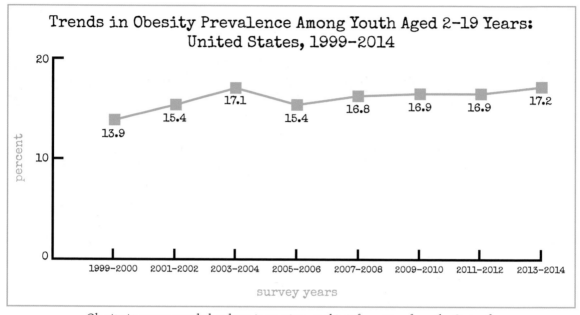

Obesity in young people has been increasing, as this information from the State of Obesity project shows.

How Do We Gain Weight?

Children and adults in the United States are becoming over-weight because they consume more calories than they burn off in physical activity. Calories are the units used to measure the energy the body gets from food. This energy keeps people alive and moving and keeps children growing. However, when calo-rie intake is too high, excess food calories are stored as fat, and people gain weight.

As anyone who has tried to lose weight knows, the human body is more efficient at gaining weight than losing it. Scientists say this is the product of thousands of years of human history. Ancient humans were hunter-gatherers who spent their days

"Good" Versus "Bad" Fat and Carbs

The human body needs dietary fat for energy, but most Americans eat far more fat than their bodies can use. Some types of fat are worse for people's health than others. Saturated fat is present in meats such as beef, pork, and lamb, and it is also in butter, cream cheese, mayonnaise, and salad dressing. Too much saturated fat boosts the "bad" cholesterol in the body and increases the risk of heart disease.

Trans fat is also closely linked to heart disease and obesity. It is a solid fat found in dairy and meat products, but it is also used heavily in packaged and fried foods. It is often listed on food labels as hydrogenated vegetable oil. Food producers make trans fat by altering vegetable oils through a process called hydrogenation. They use it because products made with it have a longer shelf life than products made with other fats. Nutritionists advise that people should consume healthier fats instead, such as those found in olive oil, peanut oil, and avocado oil.

Carbohydrates, commonly called "carbs," come in two main forms: sugars and starches. When people load up on carbs by eating snack foods, soda, and doughnuts, they are likely to gain weight. However, the carbs in fruits and whole grains provide energy for physical activity and deliver important nutrients to the body.

doing intense physical activity. In harsh conditions or when food was scarce, they were forced to go for days or weeks at a time with barely enough food to sustain them. Those who could store food as body fat most efficiently when food was plentiful had a genetic advantage, because that excess fat could be converted to energy during the leaner times to keep them alive.

The result is that the body is genetically programmed to protect against weight loss at all costs and store extra energy as fat. That is why most people do not have to worry if they skip a meal or two. The average man or woman of normal weight has enough body fat to survive for weeks or even months without food in the event of an emergency. However, the same biology that helped keep ancient humans from starving to death is poorly suited to modern conditions. Today's lifestyles are much more sedentary, and all it takes to gather food is a quick trip in the car to the supermarket. The modern environment, wrote Kelly Brownell and Katherine Battle Horgen, obesity experts and authors, "will pound you with inducements to eat, make exertion unnecessary, and do little to defend you against diseases that most threaten you."[7] The only thing that keeps most people from overeating, they said, is sheer willpower.

Obesity and Health Risks

For those who overeat and gain weight to the point of obesity, the health risks are often serious. Studies confirm that obesity is linked to many health problems, including arthritis, cancer, and, chief among them, heart disease. People who carry excess weight often have elevated blood pressure and cholesterol levels, both of which can lead to heart disease or stroke.

High blood pressure, also called hypertension, refers to rising pressure against the walls of blood vessels. It causes the heart to work harder and can eventually damage other organs, such as the brain and kidneys. Although some people are genetically prone to high blood pressure, the condition is aggravated by factors such as excess body fat and a sedentary lifestyle.

A GROWING PROBLEM

"Obesity, diabetes, and other diseases caused by poor diet and sedentary lifestyle now affect the health, happiness, and vitality of millions of men, women, and, most tragically, children and pose a major threat to the health care resources of the United States."
–Kelly D. Brownell and Katherine Battle Horgen, authors and obesity experts

Kelly D. Brownell and Katherine Battle Horgen, *Food Fight: The Inside Story of the Food Industry, America's Obesity Crisis, & What We Can Do About It.* Chicago, IL: McGraw-Hill Contemporary Books, 2004, p. 3.

People who eat a diet high in fat and low in dietary fiber (which comes from foods such as fruits and vegetables) are also at risk for developing high LDL, or so-called bad cholesterol, levels. LDL deposits form on the walls of arteries, making it harder for the heart to pump blood, and this, too, boosts the chances of heart disease.

Diabetes is another serious illness that is closely tied to obesity. In simple terms, it is a condition in which the body has difficulty turning food into energy. Diabetes takes two forms, type 1 and type 2. Type 1 most often occurs in children and teens and is typically inherited. Type 2, on the other hand, generally develops later in life and is linked to factors such as excess weight gain, an unhealthy diet, and a sedentary lifestyle. Both types of diabetes involve problems in the way the body processes glucose, a sugar that comes from carbohydrates. Glucose is the body's main source of fuel. It provides the energy for every thought or movement humans make. However, to use glucose, the body must first have a hormone called insulin, which is produced in the pancreas.

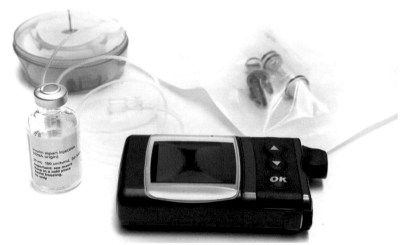

If the body is unable to produce insulin or becomes resistant to it, a person must get insulin from an outside source, generally either through injection or a pump (shown here).

In type 1 diabetes, the body is unable to make insulin. In type 2, the body produces insulin, but it either makes too little of it or it becomes resistant to it. The glucose accumulates in the blood, which causes blood sugar levels to rise dangerously high, damaging tissues and blood vessels. As of 2017, diabetes is the seventh-leading cause of death in the United States.

In recent years, the rate of type 2 diabetes in the United States has soared along with the rate of obesity. About 1.4 million new diabetes cases are diagnosed in U.S. adults each year. In adults ages 20 and older, more than 1 in every 10 people has diabetes, and in people ages 65 and older, that rate is more than 1 in 4. Health experts warn that more than twice as many people may have higher than normal blood sugar levels, a sign that they are at risk for developing the disease. Minority groups with high rates of obesity have been particularly hard hit. Hispanics have a 12.8 percent increased risk of diabetes, and non-Hispanic blacks have a 13.2 percent increased risk than non-Hispanic white adults in the United States. Asian Americans have a 9 percent higher risk of diabetes. Fortunately, the CDC reported in 2015 that although type 2 diabetes is still much more common than it was in the 1990s, the rate has begun to decline. This is likely due to people recognizing the impact of their unhealthy diet and exercise habits and implementing long-term lifestyle changes. However, this only applies to people who can afford to eat healthier and exercise more, which may be why the rates for blacks and Hispanics have not changed as dramatically as those for whites.

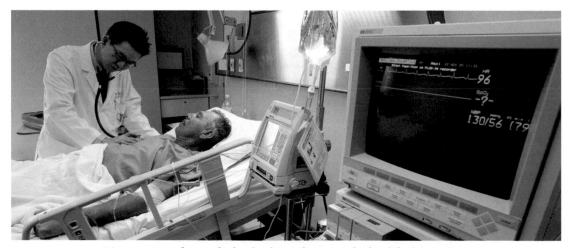

Many overweight people develop heart disease and other life-threatening health problems.

Can Obesity Be Genetic?

Some people have no trouble staying thin, while others struggle to lose weight and keep it off. Modern humans have all inherited the same basic biology, but some may be genetically more prone to obesity. Genes affect metabolism—the rate at which people convert food into energy. They determine whether bodies put on fat easily or resist fat loss. They also play a role in the nervous energy, restless pacing, and other unconscious activities that help some people burn calories more readily than others.

Genes may also help to explain the high rate of obesity and diabetes among some racial groups in America. The ancient ancestors of African American and some Native American groups lived in harsh conditions where starvation loomed as a constant threat. Scientists suggest that their descendants may have inherited a "thrifty genotype," a genetic makeup that helped people obtain extra energy from small amounts of food and store away fat. This genotype was critical to survival in ancient times, but it may make people more prone to obesity now that food is readily available in supermarkets, restaurants, drive-through windows, and vending machines.

Emotional Effects

Diabetes and other health risks associated with obesity are serious, but the emotional and psychological damage caused by obesity cannot be ignored. American culture idolizes super-thin models and celebrities. Advertisers target consumers with images that make many people dissatisfied with their bodies. Diet and weight advice is everywhere in magazines, best-selling books, and TV talk shows. In a society that places so much emphasis on staying slender, people who are obese often experience shame, anxiety, or depression. Some extremely overweight people become caught in a vicious cycle in which they feel depressed or angry and then eat for emotional reasons to feel better, only to end up feeling worse. Others become so desperate to lose weight that they fall prey to dangerous weight-loss schemes and diet pills or develop dangerous eating disorders that take a toll on their physical health.

Obesity can also have a devastating impact on social lives, marriages, and academic and professional opportunities. Obese job applicants often recount having encouraging conversations with potential employers over the phone but then being quickly dismissed when they appear in person for a job interview. One study examined the effects of obesity on economic status and found that obese women, in particular, were more likely to have lower-paying jobs or to be unemployed than those with BMIs in the normal range. They were also more likely to marry men with lower incomes.

For overweight children, the psychological harm inflicted by relentless teasing, bullying, and social stigmatization can lead to a lifetime of body hatred, low self-esteem, anxiety, and depression. Extremely overweight children may be repeatedly excluded from social groups, sports teams, or birthday parties. Some refuse to take part in physical education (PE) classes or other sports activities for fear of being teased or bullied. Others develop eating disorders or become "yo-yo dieters," constantly losing weight and then gaining it back again.

Weight Study Discrepancies

Despite the evidence that obesity is linked to serious health and emotional risks, some critics argue that the warnings about an obesity epidemic in the United States are exaggerated. They say the nation is obsessed with dieting and weight loss for cosmetic rather than legitimate health reasons. "Americans are enjoying longer lives and better health than ever before," wrote Paul Campos, the author of *The Obesity Myth*. "The claim that four out of five of us are running serious health risks because of our weight sounds exactly like the sort of exaggeration that can produce a cultural epidemic of fear, bearing no relation to any rational assessment of risk."[8]

At the center of this debate are studies in which scientists have attempted to link obesity to early death. Identifying such a link is difficult, however, because death certificates list the

Many people say that a sedentary lifestyle has caused the obesity epidemic, but others say that warnings are blown out of proportion.

disease that is the immediate cause of death, such as diabetes or heart failure, and rarely mention obesity. This forces scientists to rely on surveys and make educated guesses about how many deaths are directly related to excess weight gain.

In March 2004, controversy erupted with the release of a widely publicized CDC report that claimed that as many as 400,000 deaths every year in the United States could be linked to obesity, making it the second leading cause of death after cigarette smoking. Media coverage of the obesity crisis exploded.

IS THIS ONLY HAPPENING IN AMERICA?

"The American experience merely parallels what is happening all over the world; economic development invariably leads to less malnutrition, a more sedentary lifestyle, higher rates of obesity—and far longer life expectancy."–Paul Campos, author

Paul Campos, *The Obesity Myth: Why America's Obsession with Weight Is Hazardous to Your Health.*
New York, NY: Gotham, 2004, p. 122.

However, just a year later, the CDC admitted that the methods used in the study were flawed and revised the number of annual obesity-related deaths dramatically downward—first to 365,000, then to 112,000. The revised report even suggested that modestly overweight people may live longer on average than those in the normal or underweight BMI ranges. Groups representing the food industry were quick to comment on the new results. A spokesman for the industry group Center for Consumer Freedom wrote, "While government officials insist America is suffering from an epidemic of obesity, it's more like an epidemic of obesity myths."[9]

Health advocates such as Brownell and Battle Horgen caution that people should not focus on the controversy over obesity-related deaths and lose sight of the larger problem. They say that obesity did not become a critical issue simply because it has been hyped in the media. It is of major concern because millions of people are affected by it, its health and emotional effects are serious, treatments are costly and often do not work, and the behaviors linked to it—lack of physical activity and poor eating habits—are themselves contributors to poor health.

CHAPTER 2

What Causes American Obesity?

A merica has the largest percentage of overweight people out of any country in the world, but why are Americans overweight? French food is known for its rich, creamy desserts and sauces. A popular German dish called spätzle is made by frying egg noodles in butter. In many Dutch cities, street vendors sell cones of French fries with a hearty dipping sauce made mainly of mayonnaise. While these countries enjoy foods high in calories and fat, few diet books make the best-seller list, few people eat frozen dinners with names such as "Lean Cuisine," and some grocery stores do not even stock fat-free milk. However, the obesity rates in European countries are lower than the growing rate in America, and European visitors are often shocked by the large number of obese Americans they see.

Fast food and culture in America are having a huge effect on the way people buy and consume food throughout the world. Most countries are familiar with companies such as McDonald's, Coca-Cola, and Lay's, yet in America, a unique mix of social media and cultural forces encourage people to eat more; this has dramatically altered their diets and lifestyles. America's food industry is immensely profitable and spends billions of dollars marketing its products so that Americans will spend more time in front of TVs and computer screens and on their phones. Many people say that Americans live in a culture where it is hard not to become overweight.

Too Many Choices?

The abundance of food is a major factor in the nation's growing weight problem. There is a greater quantity and variety of food today in the United States than in any other culture in the history of the world. In 2015, there was an average of 39,500 items available in a supermarket, compared to close to 500 a century ago. A visit to almost any local supermarket in the United States makes this readily apparent. These markets carry 12 times as many different food products as they did in the early 1960s. Shelves are lined with row after row of packaged foods, including snack items, sliced and shredded cheeses, yogurts with toppings and mix-ins, sugary breakfast cereals, and creamy frozen desserts. There are dozens of varieties of Oreo cookies and more than 30 types of Lay's chips.

Americans like to have choices, but some experts say there are too many options in grocery stores and supermarkets.

Food is plentiful in America almost 24 hours a day, not only in supermarkets but also at shopping malls, airports, stadiums, drugstores, museums, and even schools and hospitals. Across the country, food can be purchased within short driving distances of most neighborhoods and along highway exits at convenience stores, gas stations, and fast food restaurants. The U.S.

Department of Agriculture (USDA) estimated that when all the food currently available to the American public is divided by the total number of people in the country, the nation is producing more food per resident than ever before. Americans are also eating more than ever before. Studies of Americans' diets as well as data on the total number of calories in the food supply show a marked increase in consumption in every major food group since the 1970s.

Packaged and Processed Problems

One of the most striking changes in Americans' eating habits is that they snack far more than in previous decades. According to food industry data, Americans average 20 food contacts, or number of times they eat something, per person each day, including snacks and meals. In contrast, the French average seven food contacts per person each day. This is largely due to the introduction of thousands of packaged and processed, or manufactured, food products into the U.S. market. These foods are designed for convenience. They are available in single-serving–size packages or microwavable containers. They can be gulped down, often without a fork and spoon, in the car, at an office desk, or between classes at school. They include drinkable yogurts, cereal bars, potato chips, fruit snacks, and lunches ready to go straight to school without any kitchen preparation time. Snack foods are becoming the number one selling grocery category in the country.

FOODS VERSUS HABITS

"There are no good or bad foods, only good or bad diets or eating styles. No single food or type of food ensures good health, just as no single food or type of food is necessarily detrimental to health."
—American Dietetic Association

The American Dietetic Association, "Total Diet Approach to Communicating Food and Nutrition Information," position paper, 2002. www.eatright.org/cps/rde/xchg/ada/hs.xsl/advocacy_adar_0102_ENU_HTML.htm.

The Snack Food Association, an industry group representing hundreds of U.S. companies that manufacture and supply snack food items, estimates that Americans buy more than $124 billion worth of snack foods each year.

Because they are so convenient to consume, these processed snacks and other food items have replaced fresh fruits, vegetables, and whole grains in many Americans' diets. People increasingly eat processed cheese and cheese spreads, many of which contain little or no real cheese, and French fries and potato chips instead of unprocessed potatoes. Processed foods are not just convenient, they also seem to offer good value for the dollar in comparison to fresh produce, fish, or meat, which can be expensive and time-consuming to prepare. For low-income Americans who live in communities where there are few, if any, grocery stores, processed foods may be their only choice. There may be nowhere to get fresh fruits and vegetables without traveling long distances on public transportation.

Although processed foods may seem like a bargain, nutritionists warn that they are a major contributor to rising rates of obesity. Even when these foods are marketed as healthy, they are often extremely high in sugar, fat, and sodium, or salt. Processed sugars, for example, are high on the ingredients list of a wide range of packaged foods from granola bars to canned soup. In one popular kind of peanut butter, sugar is second only to roasted peanuts on the ingredients list. One brand of ketchup lists high fructose corn syrup, a sweetener that is made from cornstarch and believed to promote fat growth, as the third ingredient after tomatoes and vinegar.

When foods are processed for packaging, much of their dietary fiber is removed. Fiber is the bulky portion of plants or the starchiness in grains and beans that the body is unable to fully digest. It slows down the digestive process and makes people feel fuller and more satisfied. In many large studies, a high intake of fiber has been associated with a lower risk of heart disease. However, the more a food is processed, the more fiber is taken out of it, and the more calories are added in its place. A pound of white potatoes, for example, has only 318 calories. When that same pound of potatoes is fried in oil and processed

In many cities, unhealthy food is available right on the street. Vendors sell things such as large pretzels, sausages, soda, and hot dogs, which makes it hard for consumers to resist temptation when they walk past.

into potato chips, it has 2,500 calories. Nutritionist and author Marion Nestle said it is ironic that people in less-developed nations of the world tend to eat a healthier, higher-fiber diet than Americans because they cannot afford or do not have access to processed foods such as potato chips. Only as people become better off economically, she said, do they "abandon traditional plant-based diets and begin eating more meat, fat, and processed foods. The result is a sharp increase in obesity and related chronic diseases."[10] This is one reason why standards of beauty favored overweight and obese people in Europe in the Middle Ages: It was a sign that they were wealthy enough to afford a lot of expensive—often unhealthy—food.

A Meal of Epic Portions

Not only are Americans eating more processed foods, they are also eating more of everything else. A frequently cited reason for rising rates of obesity in the United States is the tremendous increase in portion sizes over the past few decades. Family restaurants serve up plates heaped full of food. Supermarkets and warehouse stores sell large value packs of cookies, giant boxes of cereals, and huge bricks of cheese. Food chains compete to offer the biggest meals: Burger King's Double Whopper hamburger contains two beef patties with bacon and cheese, while Denny's Lumberjack Slam breakfast comes with two pancakes, a slice of grilled ham, two strips of bacon, two sausage links, two eggs, hash browns, and two pieces of toast. Nutritionists caution that there is no longer any correlation between the size of the portions being offered and the amount of food people need to maintain healthy diets and weights.

Portion sizes in restaurants have grown over the years, and often, they offer more calories, fat, and sodium in one meal than a person should have in an entire day.

The trend toward inflated portions in the United States is driven by the fast food industry. In the 1970s, corporate officials at McDonald's discovered that they could boost sales by offering much larger portions at only slightly higher prices. The company still made a profit, because doubling the size of a cup of soda or a bag of fries added very little to its costs, and sales went up as more people were drawn to the restaurants to take advantage of the large-size bargains. All the major fast food chains soon began increasing container sizes and promoting the added value of the new supersize meals. They used terms such as "jumbo," "macho meal," and "monster" to appeal to the American view that bigger is better.

The products that the fast food chains are most likely to supersize are often loaded with fat, calories, and sodium and are low in vitamins, fiber, and other nutrients. "You're getting extra french fries, more soft drink, cheap stuff that is essentially filler," said nutrition expert Adam Drewenowski. "No one is offering you a large salad for the price of a small one."[11]

Many people avoid foods that seem extremely unhealthy but do not often think to compare the calorie count and nutritional information with other foods. When they do, they are sometimes surprised to find that foods they assumed were healthy are actually worse for them than they originally thought. For instance, in 2010, Kentucky Fried Chicken (KFC) first introduced its Double Down sandwich, a bacon cheeseburger between two pieces of fried chicken instead of buns. The sandwich had 540 calories, 32 grams (g) of fat and 1,380 milligrams (mg) of sodium. Many people were horrified by this menu item but were unaware that although it was unhealthy, other fast food menu items were even more unhealthy. A Tendercrisp Garden Salad at Burger King, which most people would assume is healthy because it is a salad, actually had more calories (670), fat (45 g) and sodium (1,740 mg) than the Double Down. This is one of the reasons people may find it difficult to lose weight: They are tricked by foods that sound healthy and do not investigate the nutritional information for themselves.

Even when people are making an effort to eat in a healthier way, they are often fooled by certain things. According to Brian Wansink, the author of *Mindless Eating*, "We overeat not because of hunger but because of family and friends, packages and plates, names and numbers, labels and lights, colors and candles, shapes and smells, distractions and distances, cupboards and containers."[12] Even when people are aware that companies use certain tricks to get people to eat more, they find it difficult to identify when these tricks are working on them.

One study performed by Wansink and his graduate students involved giving movie-goers either a medium-size or large-size bucket of extremely stale popcorn. After the movie, they asked for the buckets back and recorded how much people had eaten. Wansink's team found that even though people reported that the popcorn did not taste good and many of them had eaten lunch just before the movie, they still ate a lot of the popcorn, and those who had the large bucket ate more than those with the medium bucket. According to Wansink, the only reason people ate the popcorn was "because of all the cues around them— not only the size of the popcorn bucket, but also other factors … such as the distracting movie, the sound of people eating popcorn around them,"[13] and the idea that eating snacks at the movies makes the experience more enjoyable.

Sugary Soda

In addition to eating more food, Americans are also drinking more. Over the past 50 years, they have begun to consume huge amounts of soda, juice, beer, other alcoholic beverages, and sweetened coffees. The leading source of calories in the American diet was once white bread, but researchers report that Americans today are drinking their calories instead. Almost half of Americans report drinking soda daily, and among those who drink soda, they average about 2.6 glasses per day.

A few large and highly influential companies control most soda sales. The two biggest, Coca-Cola and PepsiCo, sell 70 percent of the carbonated beverages in the world. These companies spend hundreds of millions of dollars to market their products through TV commercials, billboards, the Internet, radio, and sponsorships of high-profile concerts, sporting events, and cultural activities. Throughout the world, the Coke and Pepsi brand names are associated with American life and popular culture.

However, the products these companies market so effectively contain no nutritional value. Soda is made with water, sugar or other sweeteners such as high fructose corn syrup, caffeine, salt,

Soda is available for purchase in every grocery store, as well as drugstores, convenience stores, and gas stations. In fact, it is hard to find a store that does not sell soda.

and chemicals. Nutritionists sometimes refer to soda as "liquid candy" because it has become the leading source of sugar in the American diet. There are roughly 10 teaspoons (49 mL) of sugar or other caloric sweeteners in a 12-ounce (.35 L) can of soda, just 2 teaspoons (10 mL) short of the maximum allotment the government recommends that Americans ingest in an entire day.

The portion sizes of soda and other high-calorie beverages have also grown enormously along with the meals they accompany. At fast food chains, coffee stores, and restaurants, a small cup has ballooned to the size that was once a medium, a medium has become a large, and the large has become gigantic. Customers who order a small soda at Wendy's, for example, get a cup filled with 16 ounces (0.47 L) of liquid. Customers who order a large soda get 40 ounces (1.18 L), which is more than a quart (0.95 L) of soda. Car manufacturers have been forced to widen car cup holders to make room for the larger 16.9-ounce (0.5 L) bot-

of soda sold in supermarkets today. However, the new cup holders are still not equipped to handle the largest of the supersize drinks. The X-Gulp, released in 2014, holds almost 2 gallons (7.57 L) of soda and has a handle to make it easier for the customer to carry.

Changing Habits and Culture: A Big Job

Fast food chains such as McDonald's and Wendy's promote soda as part of their supersize meals and sell a huge volume of it each day, yet increased soda consumption is only one of the ways in which the fast food industry has changed Americans' eating habits and lifestyles. The mass appeal and affordability of fast food restaurants allow people of all income levels to dine out more and cook less. Americans take this for granted today, but there was a time when dining out was a luxury that few people could afford. The change is generally credited to the vision of two brothers, Richard and Maurice McDonald, who opened the first McDonald's restaurant in California in 1948. The brothers put into place a revolutionary system of food preparation and service that they called the Speedee Service System. According to Schlosser, they increased efficiency and sales volume by offering a limited number of menu items, eliminating foods that required a knife or fork, and replacing glasses and dishware with paper goods. They also divided food preparation into separate tasks, assembly line–style, so that one employee spread the sauce and another wrapped the burgers in paper.

TRANSPORTING FOOD

"Many urban community dwellers would love to have better eating habits, but if there's no grocery store nearby, you're talking about getting on public transportation with a grocery cart."
–Dr. Maya Rockeymoore, president and CEO of Global Policy Solutions

Quoted in Kelly D. Brownell and Katherine Battle Horgen, *Food Fight: The Inside Story of the Food Industry, America's Obesity Crisis, & What We Can Do About It.* Chicago, IL: McGraw-Hill Contemporary Books, 2004, p. 40.

McDonald's pioneer Ray Kroc took the McDonald's Speedee Service concept to cities, suburbs, and highway exits across the nation. He created a huge chain of clean, efficient restaurants that made eating out affordable and convenient for working-class Americans and their families for the first time. Other early fast food pioneers followed his lead. Burger King, KFC, Carl's Jr., Wendy's, and other chains began to open locations across the country throughout the 1960s and early 1970s.

It would be hard to find an American who has never eaten at McDonald's.
The brand is recognized across the world as well.

Today the major fast food chains have become a familiar part of the American landscape. It is estimated that roughly a quarter of the adult population and a third of children and teens in the United States visit a fast food restaurant on any given day. In just

30 years, from the 1970s to 2001, U.S. spending on fast food expanded from $6 billion to more than $110 billion per year, and in 2015, it was reported that Americans spent more than $380 billion on fast food.

Health advocates say the tremendous popularity of fast food is a major contributor to weight gain and related illness. The all-American meals served at most fast food restaurants are extremely high in calories, fat, and sodium. In his 2004 documentary, *Super Size Me*, filmmaker Morgan Spurlock put himself on a McDonald's-only, no-exercise diet for 30 days in a row as a social experiment aimed at exposing the fast food industry's role in promoting obesity. He ate only food from McDonald's, ordered the supersize portions whenever he was asked by a McDonald's employee if he wanted to size up, and sampled every item on the menu at least once. Spurlock gained 24.5 pounds (11.1 kg) by the end of the month—almost a pound a day—and suffered from rising cholesterol levels, an inflamed liver, and heart palpitations. Food industry groups argued that few people would eat this much fast food in a single month, but although his diet was extreme, even Spurlock's doctors were surprised by the extent to which it had caused his health to decline.

"IT SHOULDN'T EVEN BE CALLED 'FOOD'"

"Fast food is terrible for you. It shouldn't even be called 'food.' It should be called more like what it is: a highly efficient delivery system for fats, carbohydrates, sugars and other bad things."
—Morgan Spurlock, writer and political activist

Morgan Spurlock, *Don't Eat This Book: Fast Food and the Supersizing of America.* New York, NY: G.P. Putnam's Sons, 2005, p. 24.

Americans' Sedentary Lifestyles

Despite the popularity of fast food, Americans might not be gaining so much weight if they were not also burning off fewer calories through physical activity than ever before. Some people argue that obesity studies focus too heavily on overeating as a cause of weight gain and ignore the equally important role played by inactivity. The United States has become one of the most sedentary cultures in the world. Simply put, Americans are not burning enough calories or staying active enough to maintain good health.

Most health experts recommend that people do more than 30 minutes of moderate physical activity 5 days a week. Children are advised to get more than one hour of physical activity each day. Moderate can mean walking slowly enough to maintain a normal conversation. However, a recent CDC study found that 80 percent of American adults fail to achieve even this minimum amount of physical activity. Even more alarming is that more than 80 million adults are completely sedentary, and they perform almost no active housework, rarely walk, and spend their leisure time sitting still.

One of the main obstacles to physical exertion is the time Americans spend sitting in their cars. The United States is a huge country, with cities and suburbs that sprawl over vast areas. Americans drive more and walk less than people in almost any other nation in the world. They commute long distances to work and drive to school, to shopping malls, and to run errands in their own communities. In many residential areas, sidewalks are rare. Many workplaces are inaccessible by public transport. According to a Harvard Health Watch study, the average American spends 101 minutes driving each day. That means the average American will spend nearly 40,000 hours of their life driving their car.

Home and work lives have also become more sedentary. Americans are quick to embrace almost any new technology that saves them time and energy. Housework once involved tremendous physical exertion—from scrubbing clothes by hand on a washboard to cleaning the oven with a scouring pad. Today, people use remote control devices to operate their televisions, stereos, and garage doors. They set the oven to self-clean and let the dishwasher scrub the pots and pans. They also increasingly spend their leisure time watching television shows or online videos, playing video games, and texting their friends.

WEIGHT DOES NOT ALWAYS DETERMINE HEALTH

"You have to remember that it doesn't take that much to be fit ... To qualify as fit, it takes about 30 minutes of walking five days a week on average. That's not a ton of caloric expenditure. It is actually quite easy physiologically to be overweight or obese, but also qualify as physically fit."—Dr. Timothy Church, chief medical officer of ACAP Health Consulting and professor of Preventive Medicine at Pennington Biomedical Research Center at Louisiana State University

Quoted in Alexandra Sifferlin, "Can You Be Fat and Fit-or Thin and Unhealthy?" *TIME*, September 5, 2012. healthland.time.com/2012/09/03/can-you-be-fat-and-fit-or-thin-and-unhealthy/.

Computers and other labor-saving devices have also transformed the American workplace. The U.S. economy today is centered on desk jobs that require little physical exertion. People are able to make phone calls, send e-mails, search reference books on the Internet, and read newspaper and magazine articles, all without getting up from their swivel chairs. In schools, children sit at their desks most of the day. In the past, they would have outdoor recess several days per week where they could run around and play. However, in 2012, *Forbes* magazine reported that in response to changing educational standards, many schools were canceling recess so children could spend more time on classwork.

Although all of these changes toward a more sedentary lifestyle are certainly making Americans more unhealthy, recent research suggests that it may not be affecting weight as much as people previously thought. Vox reported in 2016 that diet plays a much more important role in weight loss than exercise:

If a hypothetical 200-pound man added 60 minutes of medium-intensity running four days per week while keeping his calorie intake the same, and he did this for 30 days, he'd lose five pounds. "If this person decided to increase food intake or relax more to recover from the added exercise, then even less weight would be lost," [mathematician and obesity researcher Kevin Hall] added … Exercise is excellent for health; it's just not that important for weight loss. So don't expect to lose a lot of weight by ramping up physical activity alone.[14]

The article stated that researchers have found exercise burns off less than 10 to 30 percent of calories; most energy is burned off by a person's basal metabolic rate (BMR), or the energy a body uses to keep itself functioning when at rest. Genetics plays a large role in determining this rate, which means people have little control over it.

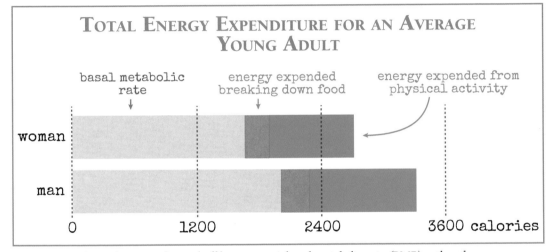

Most calories are burned off by a person's basal metabolic rate (BMR) rather than physical exercise, as this information from Vox shows.

Nature Versus Nurture

This trend toward a more sedentary lifestyle at work and home affects Americans of every income level and racial group. People of all backgrounds are eating more and exercising less. Although they have all inherited the same basic human biology, some people remain thin while others become obese. Scientists believe genetic factors may play a role. A child with severely overweight parents has a high likelihood of becoming overweight too. Studies also show that the BMIs of adopted children tend to match more closely to their biological parents than their adoptive parents.

A Cultural Shift

In one of New York City's Chinese neighborhoods, recent immigrants flock to traditional markets to buy poultry, Chinese cabbage, bean sprouts, and other fresh vegetables. They sip from bowls of steaming broth at nearby noodle shops and prepare traditional meals at home for their families. Their children, however, frequently reject these foods in favor of hamburgers, soda, pizza, and candy. "At home we would shop in the open market," Jian Kang Qiu, a 43-year-old immigrant from China's Guangdong province, told a *New York Times* reporter in 2006. "There was not so much packaged food. We would eat maybe two meals a day. Rice with something on the side, fish or vegetables."[1] However, after just six years in the United States, Qiu and his family were eating a diet high in fat, processed sugar, and sodium. Qiu's mother and sister were diagnosed with type 2 diabetes. Qiu has given up trying to control what his teenage daughter eats. "She would prefer American food," he said. "Her friends are going for pizza, she wants to go for pizza."[2]

1. Quoted in Marc Santora, "East Meets West, Adding Pounds and Peril," *New York Times*, January 12, 2006, National Desk, p. 1.
2. Quoted in Santora, "East Meets West."

Genetic factors alone, however, cannot account for the rapid rise of weight gain and obesity in the United States. The human gene pool changes very gradually, over thousands of years. Obesity rates in the United States have nearly doubled in less than 30 years. Scientists suggest that when people who are genetically prone to weight gain are exposed to environmental conditions in which high-calorie foods are plentiful—as they are in the United States today—they are more likely to become obese. When someone with a low BMR eats a lot of food or food that is high in calories, they are more at risk for gaining weight than someone with a high BMR. "Biology is important,"

Brownell and Battle Horgen wrote, "but the environment steals the show."[15]

Some of the most compelling evidence that obesity is closely tied to environment comes from the experience of immigrant groups living in the United States. A large-scale study of more than 32,000 people who responded to a national health survey—14 percent of them immigrants—found that obesity is rare until they have lived in the United States for more than 10 years. About 8 percent of immigrants who lived in the country for less than a year were obese, but that increased to 19 percent for those who had lived in the country for at least 15 years. Even researchers who suspected that people would gain weight as they adopted the eating habits and lifestyles of their new country were surprised by the magnitude of the change. "The very act of living in the United States," said *The Fat of the Land* author Michael Fumento, "puts you at greater risk for obesity."[16]

Children's and Teenagers' Eating Habits and Lifestyle

Young people see food around them all the time, and they have not yet learned all the tricks companies use to get people to eat more. Therefore, they often take their cues about eating from the people around them. If an adult expresses a distaste for vegetables, a child will be more likely to reject them as well. Additionally, the eating habits of both adults and children are influenced by the size of the plate or container food comes in. Wansink conducted a study where five-year-olds at a day care were given a few cookies either on a plate or in a plastic bag. The ones who got the plate believed the plate could be refilled and wanted more cookies, while the ones who got the bag believed all the cookies were gone and were satisfied with the amount they received. Following these kinds of cues can make it easier for people to put on weight, so it is important for them to learn from a young age how to think about what they are eating as well as how much they eat throughout the day.

At the same time that they are eating more, children and teenagers are also burning fewer calories. Television streaming services, movies, video games, cell phones, and computers keep them sitting still for hours at a time. In many communities, they have little time for informal, active play and are often driven to school, activities, and meetings with friends. The result is that the majority of U.S. children fail to meet the exercise and dietary guidelines recommended by the USDA to grow and maintain healthy bodies.

Young People's Weight

The rates of obesity and being overweight in U.S. children of all races, ages, and genders are climbing rapidly. Until the 1960s, the combined rate remained steady at around 5 or 6 percent

Kids often choose unhealthy fast food options, such as burgers and soda, instead of healthy meal options.

of young people, but by the year 2010, around one-third of children ages 6 to 19 were classified as overweight or obese. The average 10-year-old boy or girl in the United States today weighs approximately 7 to 13 pounds (3 to 5 kg) more than a child the same age did in the 1980s. The percentage of overweight black, Native American, and Latinx children, as well as lower-income people of any race, is significantly higher than that of middle- and upper-income white children.

Health officials say the rising percentage of overweight children is deeply troubling but that it is also important to keep the numbers in perspective. The vast majority of children still fall in the normal weight range. Even among young children who are overweight, there may not be cause for concern. Long-term studies suggest that most overweight five- or seven-year-olds do not become obese adults.

However, for children who are severely overweight or those who are overweight as adolescents, the health risks are serious and sometimes life threatening. Most of the severely obese adults in the country were first overweight as teenagers. This is especially true for women. Extremely overweight children and teens are at great risk for health problems such as heart disease, high blood pressure, asthma, and obstructive sleep apnea, a dangerous condition in which they experience interrupted breathing during sleep. In the largest study of children's health of its kind in the world, researchers at Tulane University tracked thousands of children in the racially mixed, semirural community of Bogalusa, Louisiana. They looked for early warning signs of heart disease and high blood pressure and discovered that more than 60 percent of overweight children between 5 and 10 years old had already developed at least one risk factor for heart disease.

Overweight children also have a higher risk of type 2 diabetes. For decades, doctors believed that type 2 diabetes, once called adult-onset diabetes, was a disease of aging that progressed gradually as the cells of the body became less sensitive to insulin. However, that changed with the rise of childhood obesity, as more children began arriving at hospitals and clinics with alarmingly high blood sugar levels. A genetic predisposition to diabetes tends to run in families, but the disease is clearly linked to excess weight and a lack of physical activity. It is estimated that one out of every three American children born in the year 2000 will get the disease at some time in their lives. In fact, more than 200,000 children have been diagnosed with diabetes already, and the number continues to grow. For poor and minority children, the risk is even greater.

What Do Kids Eat?

Scientists believe that obesity-related diseases such as type 2 diabetes are occurring frequently in childtren today primarily because young people in the United States are consuming so

Many kids spend a lot of time sitting. This sedentary lifestyle contributes to developing diseases such as type 2 diabetes.

much high-calorie, sugary, and fat-laden junk food. The USDA guidelines advise that children eat a balanced diet heavy in nutrient-dense foods and beverages from each of the five food groups, which include grains, vegetables, fruits, protein, and dairy. Most children, however, fall far short of meeting these guidelines. For example, the guidelines recommend that children consume at least 5 servings (roughly 2.5 cups) of fruits and vegetables per day. However, 6 in 10 children do not eat the amount of fruit that is recommended per day, and the number jumps to 9 in 10 children for vegetables. Of the vegetables children do consume, about a third take the form of white potatoes, while almost half of the fruit comes from sweetened fruit juice. When poor children's diets are evaluated, researchers find that their eating habits are even worse.

Although potato chips, sweetened fruit juice, and other processed and packaged foods supply the calories children need to grow and develop, they lack vital nutrients. They are also loaded with sugar and saturated or trans fats. Americans often feed processed sugar to their babies and young children. A jar of Heinz custard pudding baby food, for example, contains nearly

4 teaspoons (19.7 mL) of sugar, roughly the amount that can be found in the same size serving of soda. Breakfast cereals that are marketed to very young children are full of processed sugar. Even parents who try to keep sugary and salty junk foods out of the hands of their young children are forced to fight the nation's food culture. "Parents must compete with television, movies, candy fundraisers, schools filled with soft drinks, snack foods, and fast foods, and peer pressure to eat,"[17] Brownell and Battle Horgen wrote.

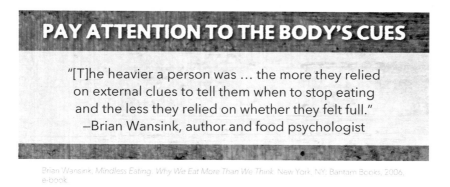

PAY ATTENTION TO THE BODY'S CUES

"[T]he heavier a person was ... the more they relied on external clues to tell them when to stop eating and the less they relied on whether they felt full."
—Brian Wansink, author and food psychologist

Brian Wansink, Mindless Eating: Why We Eat More Than We Think. New York, NY: Bantam Books, 2006, e-book.

As children grow older and enter school, their eating habits become worse. School-age kids pack potato chips, crackers, cheese puffs, sugar-laden yogurt, muffins, and candy for lunch and snacks. They also consume several servings of sweetened beverages such as soda, chocolate milk, or artificial fruit drinks each day. They snack on chips at baseball and soccer games and celebrate victory with their teammates at Pizza Hut and McDonald's.

American teenagers consume many of the same unhealthy processed and packaged foods as younger children but generally in much larger amounts. They eat few servings of fruits or green vegetables and purchase many of their meals away from home, often at fast food chains. They also drink huge amounts of soda and sweetened fruit drinks. According to a report by the non-profit nutrition and health advocacy group Center for Science in the Public Interest (CSPI), the average teenage boy drinks two cans of soda a day, almost triple the amount consumed 20 years ago. Additionally, about one in four teenagers reports drinking soda every day. According to the Harvard T. H. Chan School of Public Health, "Sugary drinks (soda, energy, sports drinks) are the top calorie source in teens' diets (226 calories per day), beating out pizza (213 calories per day)."[18]

With so many options to choose from, it is no wonder that soda is such a popular beverage choice for young adults.

American children of all ages also eat out more frequently than in the past at fast food chains and family-style restaurants, where they order not only soda but also portions that contain nearly double the food calories that they would normally consume at home. CSPI researched menus from thousands of kids' meals, and their results revealed that some meals contained over 1,000 calories, when the recommended number of calories children ages 4 to 10 should be eating for the whole day is between 1,200 and 2,200. They also found that of the restaurants analyzed, 83 percent served fried chicken, such as chicken nuggets or chicken fingers, in the kids' meal, and 65 percent served hamburgers. These foods are high in fat and calories.

WEIGHT LOSS AND METABOLISM

"[Weight loss slows down metabolism, so the] body goes from being like a truck, burning a lot of fuel, to being more like a Prius, burning less gas to go the same distance, when you've lost weight."
–J. Graham Thomas, assistant professor of psychiatry and human behavior at the Weight Control & Diabetes Research Center of the Miriam Hospital in Providence, Rhode Island

Quoted in Rachael Rettner, "The Best Way to Keep Weight Off," LiveScience, February 26, 2016. www.livescience.com/53863-best-way-keep-weight-off.html.

Small Consumers

The decline in quality of children's eating habits in the United States comes at a time when there is a huge increase in food marketing aimed directly at children and teens. On TV, on the Internet, on billboards, in vending machines, and in supermarkets and toy stores—almost everywhere that children turn—they are exposed to ads for high-calorie foods. The food industry spends more than $1.6 billion each year on marketing aimed at persuading U.S. children to consume more food products, and in 2012, fast food restaurants spent $4.6 billion in total on all advertising. They hire consultants who specialize in devising clever new ways to give these products maximum kid appeal.

For food companies looking to boost their profits, children represent a winning combination. They not only have tremendous influence over their families' food purchases, but they are also easily persuaded by advertising. "The aim of most children's advertising is straightforward: get kids to nag their parents and nag them well,"[19] explained Schlosser.

The food marketing assault in the United States begins early in childhood. Market research has shown that a single 30-second advertisement can promote brand loyalty in children as young as age two. Repeated exposure to an ad is even more effective. Marketers appeal directly to very young children in their ads and packaging with colorful graphics and familiar characters. It is estimated that in 2012, preschoolers saw 2.8 ads for fast food per day, or 1,023 for the whole year.

Despite the growing importance of the Internet and other new technologies, television remains the medium of choice for most food marketers. Commercials for food products flood the airwaves of cable television networks that cater to children and teens, such as Nickelodeon and Cartoon Network. Advertisers have also started using Internet ads and ads within phone apps to encourage kids to convince their parents to buy their products as well.

COMPANIES SAY PARENTS PLAY A ROLE

"We want kids to buy our products. But Mom and Dad, if your kid is eating too much and eating the wrong stuff, don't let them have it."– Steve Rotter, chief creative officer of marketing company Rotter Creative Group

Quoted in Nat Ives, "The Media Business: Advertising; A Report the Possibility That Ads Contribute to Obesity in Children, the Industry Begs to Differ," *New York Times*, February 25, 2004, Business Section, p. 3.

These marketing tie-ins lure children to choose foods connected to their favorite movie or TV characters. As a result, supermarket shelves are loaded with products such as Dory macaroni and cheese, SpongeBob fruit snacks, and Scooby Doo graham crackers.

One of the hottest marketing trends in recent years is for companies to emphasize fun in their ads. They promote foods with bright colors, unusual forms and shapes, and innovative packaging. Marketers call this phenomenon "eatertainment." "Food commercials aimed at children don't talk as much about 'great taste' as they do about having fun—associating food with action, friends, excitement," wrote Susan Linn, author of *Consuming Kids*. "None of these are good reasons for eating."[20]

Bright, well-placed ads encourage children to beg their parents to eat at fast food restaurants.

Marketing to Youth

Fast food companies also aggressively target children in their marketing. McDonald's pioneer Ray Kroc recognized early that children were desirable customers because they generally brought parents and grandparents along with them when they visited a restaurant. The average bill for a family is three times more than that of a nonfamily transaction, so the major fast food chains work hard to make their restaurants attractive, safe, all-American places for parents and kids.

There are fast food restaurants in almost every community where children live, travel, and attend school. A 2005 study in Chicago, Illinois, found that children in nearly all the schools

Keeping the Weight Off

People who lose weight often find it difficult not to gain that weight back. Sometimes this is because they go back to their old eating habits after losing the weight, but often it is because the body tries to maintain a consistent weight; metabolism—the rate at which people burn calories—often slows down after someone loses a lot of weight because the body goes into starvation mode and begins to store extra calories. Additionally, "after weight loss, your appetite increases, you have to eat more to feel satiated and you may increase your preference for higher calorie foods, according to a 2015 review paper from a government-backed panel of weight-loss experts."[1]

People who are most successful in keeping weight off after they have lost it tend to have the same habits. They get enough sleep at night, get enough exercise, find low-calorie foods they like the taste of as much as their favorite high-calorie foods, eat slowly so they can recognize when they are full, do not give up when they gain some weight back, do not skip meals or eat out a lot, and weigh themselves regularly so they can make adjustments to their diet and exercise routine before they gain too much weight back.

1 Rachael Rettner, "The Best Way to Keep Weight Off," Live Science, February 26, 2016. www.livescience.com/53863-best-way-keep-weight-off.html.

in the city were only a 10-minute walk from at least 1 fast food chain. There are fast food franchises at stadiums, movie theaters, suburban mini malls, and even children's hospitals. Still, companies such as McDonald's and Burger King do not leave anything to chance. They spend millions of dollars on advertising to ensure that young people walk through their doors.

Fast food companies aggressively market to children in other ways too. McDonald's operates close to 8,000 play areas, more than any other private company in the United States, and the company encourages kids to have birthday parties there. These colorful play spaces are highly effective in attracting families with young children. In some low-income, inner-city neighborhoods where there are few clean, safe public parks or playgrounds, a fast food play area may be the only place where parents feel comfortable bringing young children to play.

Fast food companies also entice children with toys and characters linked to their favorite movies, TV shows, and sports teams. McDonald's is one of the largest toy distributors in the nation. A popular toy promotion can easily double or even triple weekly sales of the company's children's meals. In 1997, for example, McDonald's launched the Teenie Beanie Baby campaign, one of the most successful marketing efforts in U.S. advertising history. At the time, McDonald's normally sold around 10 million Happy Meals per week. During 10 days in April 1997, when the chain included a Teenie Beanie Baby with each purchase, sales skyrocketed to 100 million Happy Meals.

When measured by the number of U.S. children who regularly eat at a fast food restaurant, these marketing strategies are a resounding success. On a typical day, one-third of U.S. children consume a fast food meal, and about one-third of American children eat fast food or pizza every day. Every month, more than 90 percent of American children ages 3 to 9 visit a McDonald's restaurant. However, the children's meals at these restaurants are loaded with fat, sodium, sugar, and calories. "They [fast food chains] don't think about nutrition if it interferes with profits,"[21] *Diabesity* author Francine R. Kaufman wrote.

However, beginning in 2011, McDonald's realized that customers' increased worries about obesity would affect its profits if it did not start serving healthier food. It began offering lower-calorie salads as well as apples instead of fries with Happy Meals. Other fast food restaurants soon began offering healthier options as well. Most Americans still associate fast food restaurants with unhealthy food, though, and although a salad is often healthier than a hamburger, restaurants increase the calories by adding cheese or other high-calorie foods, so they are not as healthy as a salad containing only vegetables that someone might make at home. The healthier options may have stopped some customers from completely abandoning fast food restaurants, but they have not greatly increased sales.

McDonald's frequently uses cartoon characters, such as Mario and Luigi, to promote their Happy Meals, which also come with a toy.

Exercise on the Decline

At the same time that U.S. children are indulging in more snacks and fast food, they are also exerting themselves less. The evidence is overwhelming that when inactivity is combined with diets high in fat and sugar, the risk of obesity grows. Although exercise must be combined with a low-calorie diet to provide effective weight loss, it is still a good way to prevent heart disease, diabetes, and other illnesses, as well as keep muscles strong. However, children and teens in the United States today belong to the most sedentary generation in history.

Some health experts blame television, the Internet, and video games for children's lack of physical fitness. American children spend more time online than doing anything else except sleeping. Children who spend excessive time in front of computer or phone screens tend to engage in active play less than their peers who spend less time online, although some studies suggest that teens who are not watching might still be inactive—playing board games or reading. They are also exposed to hundreds of ads that prompt them to snack while they sit.

Overweight Since Age 12

Obese teenagers often suffer from anxiety and depression. They may feel isolated and hopeless and blame themselves for failing to lose weight. A severely obese 17-year-old girl from Rochester, New York, related her story on the American Obesity Association website:

I've been overweight since I was 12 years old. I used to go to school, but I had to drop out because people continued to make fun of me.

I suffer from depression, anxiety and agoraphobia [fear of public spaces that are not easy to escape from quickly]. I hate my body so much and I wish I could lose all this weight in a heartbeat, but I can't. Now I sit around in the house all day, and when I do go out I don't even get out of the car. I joined a gym, but I don't know what good that's going to do.

I missed my whole teenage-hood because of my obesity ... I feel so guilty for letting myself get so big and I wish I could just live an ordinary teenage life ... I really need some support right now.[1]

With so many messages about looking thin and beautiful being seen daily in TV, magazine, Internet, and billboard ads, it is no wonder many overweight and obese people feel anxious and depressed. However, having a positive attitude toward themselves and the process of creating long-term, healthy lifestyle changes can give people who are seeking to lose weight a better chance at success.

1. Quoted in Dr. Peter Owens, *Teens, Health & Obesity*, Broomall, PA: Mason Crest, 2014.

Physical activity is on a downward slide for other reasons, too. Children in the United States walk and ride their bikes far less than in previous decades. The National Transportation Board estimated that roughly 48 percent of children in 1969 walked or biked to school. By 2009, that number had fallen to just 13 percent. In many suburbs, schools are out of walking range or located across busy streets and highways. Parents are reluctant to let children walk because they fear for their safety. The problem is worse in many low-income communities with high crime rates, where it is sometimes dangerous for children to be out on the streets at certain hours of the day. In many of these same communities, parks and playgrounds have fallen into disrepair or are considered unsafe for play.

Even the country's growing number of youth soccer, baseball, hockey, tennis, gymnastics, and other organized sports leagues are out of reach for many American children. These have replaced casual play and pickup games in many places, but they are expensive to start and maintain and require heavy parent involvement. They also tend to become highly competitive as children grow older. As a result, children who are less confident about their athletic abilities are likely to drop out of these leagues by their teenage years and are left with few other outlets for physical activity. Many people do not exercise at all by the time they reach age 18 or 19.

This trend toward sedentary living is even worse for girls than for boys. American popular culture stresses appearance, thinness, and glamour for girls, rather than athletic skill, fitness, or overall health. When the media does focus on girls in sports, the messages are often confusing. Stories about female athletes tend to emphasize appearance or femininity rather than athleticism, so girls may move less while playing sports in order to avoid sweating too much. They may even attempt to avoid physical activity completely. One study by Professor Alan Donnelly of the Centre for Physical Activity and Health Research at the University of Limerick in Ireland found that teenage girls spend an average of 19 hours per day sitting or lying down. This increases their risk of developing various health problems as well as gaining weight.

The Role of Schools

Many children and teens are not exercising at school, either. Because schools are often crowded, in need of money, and under pressure to improve academic standards and test scores, physical fitness has become a low priority. In fact, many school systems have abandoned the requirement for physical education altogether. A survey by the CDC found that the percentage of U.S. students who attended daily PE classes in high school declined from 42 percent in 1991 to 29 percent in 2013. The percentages were even lower in mainly black and Latinx school districts, which often lack the money and resources to keep PE programs going. Even when schools do offer traditional gym classes, they tend to favor children who are the most athletic and coordinated. Kids who are overweight or less coordinated than their peers often end up on the sidelines. "If you're a bit clumsy, a bit uncoordinated, a bit self-conscious—you're left out,"[22] said Reginald Washington, chief medical officer at Rocky Mountain Hospital for Children.

Just because schools are required to serve vegetables, fruits, and whole grains does not mean that students will choose to eat them.

Although schools are now required to follow strict guidelines for lunches and snacks, people may argue that students still do not make healthy choices when it comes to school lunches. Schools may be required to serve vegetables, fruits, and whole grains, but students often do not eat the vegetables given to them and instead opt to buy two slices of pizza to fill up instead. For this reason, it is important to help people understand from a young age the important role diet plays in weight management and the tricks companies use to encourage people to buy their food.

CHAPTER 4

The Food Industry's Role in Obesity

Many people have begun to demand that food manufacturers, restaurants, fast food chains, and health stores be held accountable for their role in the rising obesity rate among U.S. children and adults. This gets complicated, however, because some of the largest and most profitable companies in the world are in the food industry. Companies such as Kellogg's, McDonald's, Burger King, Coca-Cola, Kraft Food, and General Mills have a huge amount of political power and influence over American society, and much of daily life is actually influenced by these companies. Health groups often accuse these companies of ignoring medical advice and nutrition facts about the dangers of overeating high-calorie food and even say that they encourage people to eat foods they know are bad for their health. Companies accomplish this by spending millions of dollars on advertising, packaging food in oversized portions, and targeting their marketing at vulnerable groups, such as children and poor people. Increasingly, people have begun to support these targeted groups as they attempt to crack down on food industry practices.

Food industry groups argue that attempts to control and monitor the sale of food and soda are misguided. They say the United States is a free-market economy, which means that consumers must take responsibility for their own food choices. Although some food companies have changed their menus to include healthier options and display calorie counts, critics still believe that this is not enough. With Americans' long-term health at stake, they believe that society must intervene to make major changes to the way the food industry does business.

Using the Tobacco Industry as a Model

Health advocates often cite the nation's successful campaign against cigarette smoking as a model of how to battle the powerful food and soda industries. In the 1980s and 1990s, the government sponsored a series of high-profile public service announcements that linked smoking to lung cancer and premature death and gave cigarettes a reputation as "death sticks." Many cities and states raised taxes on cigarettes and enacted sweeping new laws banning smoking in restaurants, bars, and public buildings. The major tobacco companies, collectively known as Big Tobacco, were pressured into accepting restrictions on advertising their products. They were also forced to pay enormous legal settlements for knowingly concealing the dangers of their products for decades and causing long-time smokers to become sick with lung cancer and other ailments.

Health and nutrition groups believe that there are many parallels between Big Tobacco and Big Food. They say that like cigarette companies, food and soda manufacturers have used misleading and aggressive advertising and other deceitful tactics to encourage people to consume products that are bad for their health. Snack products that are marketed as low fat, for example, are often high in calories and still contribute to weight gain, just as cigarettes sold as "lite" or low tar can still cause addiction. Many companies deny that their products contribute to poor health and obesity, even when research proves otherwise. Critics even

Companies use characters such as Ronald McDonald to make their food seem fun.

compare Ronald McDonald to the former Camel cigarette mascot, Joe Camel. This hip cartoon character appealed to young people and was believed to encourage them to try smoking.

"FOOD COPS"

"Like Big Tobacco, it [Big Food] characterizes critics as a conspiracy 'of food cops, health care enforcers, vegetarian activists and meddling bureaucrats' … Like Big Tobacco, it makes us believe that our freedom of choice depends directly on its freedom to garner profits."–Ellen Ruppel Shell, author and professor of science journalism at Boston University

Ellen Ruppel Shell, *The Hungry Gene: The Science of Fat and The Future of Thin.* New York, NY: Atlantic Monthly, 2002, p. 230.

Additionally, there is some evidence to prove that fat and sugar may be addictive, causing people to crave them and eat more foods that contain them. Most people are surprised to find out how many foods sugar is in; for instance, many canned soups, salad dressings, crackers, juices, dried fruits, and spaghetti sauces add sugar to improve the taste or preserve the food for a longer time. According to MSNBC, "Today, the average American consumes 22 teaspoons of sugar a day—3 times what we need."[23] Eric Stice, a neuroscientist at the Oregon Research Institute, used functional magnetic resonance imaging (fMRI) to see how people's brains reacted to sugar. His research found that many people's brains react to sugar the same way they react to addictive drugs such as cocaine, which suggests sugar may be addictive.

However, there are also many ways in which tobacco and food are different, and this may make it harder to place the blame on the food industry for rising rates of obesity. Food is critical for human survival, while smoking has no accepted health value and is not necessary to live. Selling cigarettes to minors is against the law, but selling food to them is not. The tobacco industry is dominated by a handful of companies that collectively manufacture a single product that is known to be harmful and addictive. In contrast, hundreds of food companies sell and produce many thousands of different packaged and processed snacks, desserts, cereals, dairy products, meats, and beverages. It is hard to prove that they are deliberately concealing the health risks of their products or trying to promote overeating. As a result, the American public has been reluctant to equate smoking with overeating or to apply the same strategies used against the tobacco industry to wage war against Big Food.

Restricted Marketing to Children

Health advocates believe they have the greatest chance of mobilizing public support to reform the food industry by first addressing issues such as marketing to children and junk food sales in schools. Polls show that Americans are troubled by the unhealthy food environment that surrounds children from a very young age. They are disturbed by reports of U.S. children suffering from high blood pressure and type 2 diabetes. Even those who insist that obesity and weight gain among adults should be a matter of personal responsibility often blame the food industry for exploiting children who are too young to make decisions about their long-term health.

With public support increasingly on their side, health groups and a growing number of state and federal lawmakers have begun to demand action to protect children from advertisements for junk food. Some have proposed banning TV commercials for food during the hours when children are most likely to be watching. Others insist that equal time be allotted on TV networks for the promotion of healthy foods such as fruits and vegetables, paid for with food-industry money. This is similar to a tactic used in the 1970s, when the government threatened to force cigarette manufacturers to give equal time to anti-tobacco ads. This threat led to an industry-wide agreement to end all TV advertising of cigarettes. In a 2012 report, the Federal Trade Commission (FTC), a government agency that works to prevent unfair advertising practices, noted that since 2006, many food companies have voluntarily worked to make their products healthier and advertise them in ways that promote a healthy overall diet. The report found that these changes may have contributed to children and teens making healthier food choices, such as eating more foods that are high in nutritional value and fewer foods that are high in sodium and sugar.

PORTION SIZE IS IMPORTANT

"Think of your stomach like a muscle. When it's filled with large meals three times a day, the distensibility (the scientific term for the amount your stomach walls can stretch) increases—just like your biceps would get bigger if you were working them out three times a day, [said Atif Iqbal, M.D., medical director of the Digestive Care Center at Orange Coast Memorial Medical Center]." —Rachel Nussbaum, assistant editor at Greatist

Rachel Nussbaum, "Does Your Stomach Actually Grow or Shrink Based on How Much You Eat?," Greatist, November 16, 2015. greatist.com/grow/stomach-size-eating-habits.

Public support is also growing for measures to ban the sale of soda and junk food in schools. Food and beverage sales on school campuses represent only a tiny fraction of total industry sales worldwide, but they are of great value to food companies who hope to influence children's buying habits and create loyal customers for life. In recent years, opposition to selling and promoting junk food in schools has turned into a powerful nationwide movement. Los Angeles was the first city school district to pass a soda ban, which it enacted in 2002. Starting in 2014, all school food needed to meet strict guidelines and nutrition standards to increase the amount of fruits, vegetables, and whole grains found in school lunches. Schools are also not allowed to sell soda unless it is sugar-free, and even then, the sales are regulated to only include certain age groups at certain times of the day. Food companies have lobbied hard to defeat these measures, and most were passed only after major concessions were made to industry groups. Arizona and Louisiana, for instance, give high school students a variety of choices but restrict sugary and fatty foods in the lower grades. Despite such compromises, supporters say the measures help to reverse years of poor eating habits and nutrition among American schoolchildren.

New vending machine regulations say that only healthier snacks, such as the ones shown above, can be sold in schools. Some argue that these restrictions take away people's right to make their own food choices.

Improving Food Labels

To improve eating habits among Americans of all ages, health advocates also demand greater truth in food labeling. Consumers who walk down the aisles of a grocery store encounter hundreds of packaged products whose labels proclaim they are fortified with essential vitamins, contain heart-healthy whole grains, or help reduce the risk of cancer and other diseases.

If they stop to read the ingredients lists on the packages, they often see confusing words such as dextrose, sucrose, glucose, and high fructose corn syrup, all of which are just alternate forms of processed sugar. In 1990, Louis Sullivan, then secretary of the U.S. Department of Health and Human Services, complained, "Consumers need to be linguists, scientists and mind readers to understand the many labels they see."[24]

In theory, the health claims that food companies make on their packages are supposed to be backed by firm scientific evidence, yet the federal agencies charged with overseeing food labels typically review only the most outrageous and misleading claims. This leaves food companies with tremendous freedom in how they market their products. Since consumers are eager to buy foods that protect against disease and promote longer life, companies invest heavily in research and development of products designed just so they can be marketed using health claims. For example, they fortify hundreds of foods, including sugary cereals, fruit juices, and doughnuts, with nutrients such as vitamin C, calcium, and fiber and advertise the benefits of these nutrients on their labels. In one instance, when studies suggested that a diet high in whole grains lowered the risk of heart disease, many cereal and snack companies rushed to add whole grains to their existing products. General Mills, for example, reformulated cereals such as Cocoa Puffs and Lucky Charms to contain whole grains. The company did nothing to alter the sugar or calorie content of these products, but the added whole grains meant the boxes could carry a whole-grain banner and a seal of approval from the American Heart Association. Health advocates complained that this gave consumers the false impression that the products were healthy, encouraging them to eat more.

The lack of clear labeling standards has also allowed food companies to cash in on public fears about obesity and weight gain. The 45 million Americans who are estimated to be dieting at any given time are often willing to pay extra for products that they believe will help them lose weight. Many companies have their own reduced-fat product lines that are huge moneymakers. However, nutritionists caution that low-fat and reduced-fat labels are deceiving. People tend to believe that the reduced-fat label gives them a license to eat more, but many of these products contain more added sugar and calories than the regular versions. They are just as likely to cause weight gain as any other high-calorie packaged food.

Health advocates and consumer groups want to put an end to this misleading and deceptive food labeling. They have called for a simplified format for food labels in which ingredients and nutritional content are listed in language that is easy for consumers to read and understand. They also recommend that companies be forced to use a universal definition of serving sizes so that a single serving means the same thing from one food manufacturer to the next. If the USDA determines, for example, that a single serving of soda is 8 ounces (0.24 L), then a 20-ounce (0.59 L) bottle would list 2.5 USDA servings. Advocates have proposed extending such labeling rules to restaurants, fast food chains, and vending machines as well. Many restaurants do list the calorie count next to foods to make people think twice about what they are ordering or how much they will eat. However, full nutrition

Reading food labels is important, but sometimes the labels can be confusing or misleading.

facts are often not readily available, or if they are, people often choose not to read them because if they have already decided something sounds good, they would rather not know how bad for them it is.

In 2016, National Public Radio (NPR) reported that beginning in July 2018, the Food and Drug Administration (FDA) would require an "added sugar" line on all nutrition labels so consumers can see how much sugar companies add to their products. When it was first announced, food companies such as General Mills opposed the change, claiming that it does not matter whether consumers know how much sugar is added and how much is natural, since the total will remain the same. However, Michael Jacobson, the founder of the CSPI, said "the new labels will allow consumers to make more informed choices and 'should also spur food manufacturers to add less sugar to their products.'"[25]

HOLDING THE FOOD INDUSTRY RESPONSIBLE

"Any genuine effort to reduce childhood obesity must attack the problem at its roots. And that means holding the food industry responsible for its role in creating the problem."–Susan Linn, psychologist, and Diane E. Levin, author and advocate

Susan Linn and Diane E. Levin, "Stop Marketing 'Yummy Food' to Children," *Christian Science Monitor,* June 20, 2002. www.csmonitor.com/2002/0620/p09s01-coop.html.

Taxes on Snacks and Soda

In addition to promoting new labeling standards, food-industry critics are looking to borrow a tactic from the antismoking campaign by imposing a tax on soda and junk foods. Most states currently add large taxes to packages of cigarettes, and evidence suggests that these have had a major impact in driving down the rate of smoking. Similar food taxes would force consumers to pay extra for products that promote weight gain and obesity. At least 18 states have already experimented with taxes on soda, candy, chewing gum, and other snack foods, and in 2016, major cities such as San Francisco and Oakland passed a law taxing soda. In 2014, there were 34 states with some kind of tax placed on soda sold through stores and 39 states with a tax on soda sold through vending machines. For the most part, these taxes are small and limited in scope, targeting only a few specific junk food items. Arkansas, for instance, adds a $0.02 tax on each 12-ounce (0.35 L) bottle of soda. However, promising results from Berkeley, California, showed a 20 percent decrease in the consumption of sugary drinks after a tax was imposed in 2014.

The idea of larger taxes on snack foods and soda, however, remains extremely unpopular with the majority of Americans. Many people are strongly opposed to new taxes of any kind. Taxes on food products make people think of food police interfering in people's lives and telling them what they can and cannot eat. This is widely viewed as an invasion of personal liberties and freedom of choice.

Food-industry groups have made the fight against snack and soda taxes a national priority. They have mounted aggressive ad campaigns in which they denounce junk food taxes as government interference in people's private lives. A spokesman for the industry group Center for Consumer Freedom wrote in 2002, "When we begin controlling what people can put into their mouths, there is no end to what might be next."[26]

Several states, including California and Maryland, have tried to impose large snack-food taxes despite the opposition, but these have been met with resistance from consumers. Such taxes tend to hit poor Americans the hardest, because people with lower incomes rely heavily on packaged and fast foods, especially when they have limited places to buy healthier items.

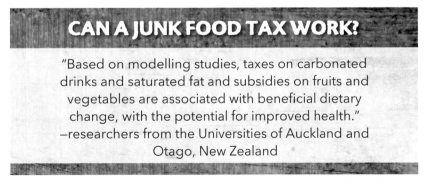

CAN A JUNK FOOD TAX WORK?

"Based on modelling studies, taxes on carbonated drinks and saturated fat and subsidies on fruits and vegetables are associated with beneficial dietary change, with the potential for improved health."
—researchers from the Universities of Auckland and Otago, New Zealand

Quoted in "Raising Junk Food Prices Could Spur People to Consume Less: Study," *Huffington Post*, December 12, 2012. www.huffingtonpost.com/2012/12/12/junk-food-prices-soda-cost-consume-less_n_2279285.html

There are also difficult questions that must be asked about which foods to tax and which to leave untaxed. In the case of the California law, grocery stores received a long list of nearly 5,000 taxable and nontaxable food items. In many cases, the distinctions between the categories seemed arbitrary. Popped popcorn was taxed; unpopped popcorn was not. Milky Way bars were taxed, but Milky Way ice-cream bars were left untaxed. The experience proved extremely frustrating to California consumers and business owners alike. They voted overwhelmingly to overturn the snack tax in 1992, just a year after it was passed. The law was changed to include candy, snack foods, and bottled water as "food products," which meant they could not be taxed, which made many people question its intent.

The failed experiment in California and other states has forced tax proponents to consider ways to make junk food taxes more acceptable. Health advocates Brownell and Battle Horgen believe that Americans are more inclined to support taxation when it is used as an incentive to encourage positive change, rather than as a deterrent to negative behaviors. They propose using tax money to help reduce prices for healthy foods such as fruits and vegetables by subsidizing them. A subsidy is when the government provides money to businesses to help them keep their prices low. This would make healthier eating more affordable for all Americans and relieve the tax burden on the poor. To eliminate the problem of unnecessary taxation, they suggest that lawmakers tax entire categories of food, such as snacks, soft drinks, and fast foods, rather than singling out specific products. They say that junk food taxes—if done right—can become an effective strategy in the fight to curb obesity.

This may be true, but Wansink's research has shown that even when the price of unhealthy food goes up, people often keep buying it. He believes an easier, quicker way for most people to lose weight gradually over time is to make small changes to the way they eat. For instance, someone who drinks a lot of soda may decide to cut back to one can per week, or make a deal with themselves to only have soda if they have also eaten broccoli that day. These types of bargains, which Wansink calls "food policies" and "food trade-offs," are specific to each individual. In order for them to be effective, people must think about what their unhealthy weaknesses are and how best to fix them. What is helpful for one person may not be helpful for another—for instance, many diet books and health guides advise people to drink less soda, but this is meaningless to someone who never drinks it at all. The best weight loss solutions are often highly personalized.

Supporters of a junk food tax suggest that candy bars are one item that should be taxed.

Lawsuits Against Fast Food Companies

Junk food taxes and food-labeling reforms are measures that must be debated in state legislatures and in Congress. Some health advocates are also prepared to take the case against Big Food to court. In 2002, two severely overweight girls in New York City made national headlines when they brought a lawsuit against McDonald's that blamed the fast food chain for their excess weight and elevated risk of disease. One of the girls, Ashley Pelman, was 14 years old at the time of the suit and weighed 170 pounds (77 kg). She had been consuming Happy Meals three to four times a week since the age of five. Jazlyn Bradley was 19 years old and weighed 270 pounds (122.5 kg). She often started the day with a McDonald's breakfast and returned to the restaurant during her lunch break and after school for a burger, fries, soda, and apple pie. The girls' lawyer argued that McDonald's food was

Choosing Who to Believe

It is often possible to find two separate studies on the same topic that seem to come to opposite conclusions. The process a study uses to collect information, the number of participants, the length of the study, and many more factors are all important in determining an accurate result. One especially important factor people need to consider is who provided the money for the study. The television show *Last Week Tonight with John Oliver* reported in 2014 that "when researchers looked at two sets of weight gain studies—one group with conflicts of interest like funding from soda companies, and one group that was independent—the vast majority of independent studies found direct links between sugar-sweetened soft drinks and weight gain or obesity, and the vast majority that weren't independent found the exact opposite of that."[1]

Unfortunately, many people do not spend the time to research studies on their own, and when faced with two studies that come to opposite conclusions, people generally choose to believe the one that reinforces a view they already hold. In other words, someone whose favorite drink is Pepsi is likely to believe a study that finds no direct link between sugar and weight gain, even if a more reliable study finds that such a link exists. In order to improve their health, sometimes people need to face painful truths and make lifestyle choices that seem difficult at first.

1. "Sugar: Last Week Tonight with John Oliver (HBO)," YouTube video, 11:34, posted by LastWeekTonight, October 26, 2014. www.youtube.com/watch?v=MepXBJjsNxs.

responsible for his clients' obesity and deteriorating health and claimed that they were entitled to damages (financial compensation).

The American public was unsympathetic. The lawsuit was denounced and ridiculed in the popular media. Late-night comedians joked about the girls' poor judgment and lack of self-control. Editorial cartoons pictured them eating at McDonald's with a gun to their heads to make the point that no one was forcing them to frequent the fast food chain against their will. In 2003, the judge dismissed the suit. He ruled that nobody was forced to eat at the restaurant and it was not the court's role to protect people from their own excesses. At the same time, he left the door open for future lawsuits against the food industry by suggesting that the case might proceed under different legal reasoning. In his ruling, he noted that McDonald's Chicken McNuggets do not contain many natural ingredients and explained that if the health dangers of such foods were not widely known, then under consumer protection laws, McDonald's would have an obligation to warn its customers.

Food-industry groups were outraged by the judge's ruling and immediately launched a nationwide counterattack. Groups such as the Center for Consumer Freedom began an intense lobbying effort to prevent lawsuits against the food industry from going forward. By 2015, 26 states, including Arizona, Colorado, Florida, Georgia, and Michigan, had enacted so-called "cheeseburger laws" that prevent people from seeking damages in court from food companies due to weight gain and associated medical conditions. In 2006, the U.S. House of Representatives passed a similar measure to prohibit such lawsuits nationwide, but the Senate did not approve the measure, so it did not become a law. Supporters of these laws say they shield businesses from having to spend huge amounts of money to defend themselves against frivolous lawsuits. However, opponents contend that there is no legitimate reason to single out the food industry for special protection under the law. "If you market products to children that cause disease, and you do it in a way that conceals the risks from parents," said Jacobson, "you may end up explaining your actions to a judge or jury. That's hardly a radical notion."[27]

The Companies' Response

The hundreds of food companies that sell and market products in the United States often respond collectively to the threat of lawsuits and policy actions through a small number of powerful groups such as the Grocery Manufacturers Association and the Center for Consumer Freedom. These industry groups vigorously deny responsibility for the obesity epidemic and appeal to patriotic values such as personal freedom and consumer choice. When they are threatened with restrictions on advertising their products, they argue that these are a violation of their constitutional right to free speech. They place the blame for childhood obesity on overly permissive parents who do not monitor their children's diets closely enough, and they suggest that sedentary lifestyles are just as much at the root of the problem as overeating. They also lash out at critics, whom they accuse of being self-appointed nannies and food cops.

However, even as these industry groups insist on their rights to freely promote their products, individual companies have begun to make voluntary changes. These companies are extremely sensitive to the charge that their marketing is to blame for childhood obesity and are eager to be seen as part of the solution. In 2005, food-industry giant Kraft, for example, announced that it would voluntarily ban advertising of some of its high-sugar products, such as Kool-Aid and Oreos, to children under 11 years old. Some fast food chains are sponsoring PE programs in schools and backing public health campaigns that focus on children's fitness.

Salads are now available on many fast food menus, but they are not always healthier than other menu items.

Health and nutrition groups view these voluntary changes on the part of food companies with skepticism. They say such efforts should be applauded, but they do not give companies a free pass to continue to engage in harmful practices such as marketing to children or promoting extra-large portions. They also complain that the healthier foods are simply an option and that unhealthy foods and drinks such as fries and soda can still be chosen. "The food industry now stands at a critical juncture and may wish to benefit from lessons learned by tobacco,"[28] Brownell and Battle Horgen have said. Food companies, in their view, have two choices: They can respond to criticism either by attacking health advocates and denying responsibility for the obesity epidemic or by acting in creative and meaningful ways to change.

CHAPTER 5

Healthy Lifestyle Changes

Americans often feel powerless to battle the large food industry or to try to change their eating habits and lifestyle, and as a result, they have become resigned to having an unhealthy relationship with food and exercise. Instead of taking a proactive approach, however, America has taken a reactive approach and focused more on treatment than prevention. Overweight Americans spend huge amounts of money, time, and energy on losing weight. They try every fad diet that comes their way, from low-carb, vegan, and high-protein to liquid-only cleanses and even chocolate diets. They support a multi-billion-dollar commercial weight-loss industry that includes companies such as Jenny Craig and Weight Watchers, and they purchase weight-loss drugs and herbal remedies that sometimes endanger their long-term health. Many people even go to the extreme, and after years of trying to lose weight, they resort to surgery. Procedures such as gastric bypass, gastrectomy, and other forms of bariatric surgery are effective for some, and they are able to dramatically change their lives. However, a greater number of patients temporarily lose the weight and then gain it back.

The problem with most fad diets is that they require drastic changes and often place strict limits on the types and amounts of foods people can have. Some are so extreme that they are unhealthy, and people on these diets lose weight too quickly, then gain it back just as quickly. According to Wansink, it is easier and healthier in the long term for people to make small, permanent adjustments in eating habits rather than large, temporary ones. He suggests limiting the number of changes to three at a time because the fewer habits people try to change at one time, the easier it is for them to succeed.

People who advocate for healthy eating say that the problem mainly lies with a culture that promotes unhealthy eating and a lack of physical activity. They believe that the nation's focus needs to shift from treatment to prevention, and that people should work to change attitudes, diets, and lifestyles that have become known as part of the American way of life. "It's not going to happen overnight," predicted former Arkansas governor Mike Huckabee, who lost 105 pounds after receiving a diagnosis of type 2 diabetes. He is working to curb obesity in his own state. "We have to believe that just as we changed attitudes toward smoking and littering and alcohol over time, we can do so [with obesity.]"[29]

Searching for a Cure

America's obesity epidemic has so far resisted easy solutions, but that has not stopped the nation's major pharmaceutical companies from pouring billions of dollars into the search for a cure or the American public from holding out hope that a quick fix or magic pill lies just around the corner. With more than 1.9 billion people worldwide reported to be either overweight or obese, drug companies are aware that there are enormous profits to be made if they can produce an effective weight-loss drug or medical treatment. The lure of enormous profits helps to explain why there are hundreds of weight-loss drugs and treatments now in the research or testing stages in labs and clinics across the country. These include drugs to regulate a hormone that controls appetite in the body, injections that produce a feeling of fullness, and implantable devices that zap electric signals to the stomach or nerve centers when a person is full. Thousands of Americans, desperate to lose weight and relieve the health symptoms and social stigma of being obese, sign up for clinical trials of these new, experimental treatments and drugs every year.

Many health advocates worry that this intensive effort to find a cure has taken away valuable resources and attention from addressing the environmental factors that promote weight gain and obesity. They say the best diet advice has not changed in decades. People who want to lose weight and keep it off must do so slowly, by eating healthier foods and smaller portions and exercising regularly. The difficulty for most people is heeding this advice in an environment that places obstacles to healthy eating and exercise at every turn.

The Dangers of Diet Drugs

Some people who are looking for a quick fix to their weight problems turn to dietary supplements that promise dramatic and long-lasting weight loss. However, these products often do not work, and sometimes they can actually endanger a person's health. Dietary supplements are not regulated by the FDA, so companies are free to put whatever they want on their labels as long as they are not making claims that their product will cure a disease. This means no one is checking to be sure that the ingredient labels are accurate or whether the products are working as promised.

The FDA does have the authority to investigate the safety of certain products, but it generally does not do this until many people have filed claims to let the FDA know a product damaged their health. By this time, it is too late for them. In one instance, a weight-loss supplement called OxyElite Pro was investigated in 2013 after more than 50 people reported problems with their livers after taking it. It was found to contain a substance called aegeline, which occurs naturally in the bael tree, a type of tree that grows in Southeast Asia. However, the form of aegeline in OxyElite Pro was synthetic—it had been made in a laboratory and may have contained other, unknown materials that were harmful to the liver. Incidents such as this prove that without regulation, it is very difficult for consumers to know what they are taking. People who assumed they were using aegeline in its natural form had no way of knowing that OxyElite Pro was actually dangerous to their health.

Making Healthier Choices

One of the first steps in combating the nation's unhealthy food environment and curbing obesity is to educate consumers to make better food choices. Many public health campaigns are already underway to help consumers read food labels,

understand portion sizes and calorie counts, and become familiar with the lifestyle and genetic factors that might put them at
higher risk for diabetes, high cholesterol, or heart disease. The
USDA recently released new dietary guidelines to help people
get the most nutrients from their calories and to ensure that they
are eating food from multiple food groups. Called MyPlate, the
guidelines also encourage people to sparingly eat foods high in
calories, fat, and processed sugar.

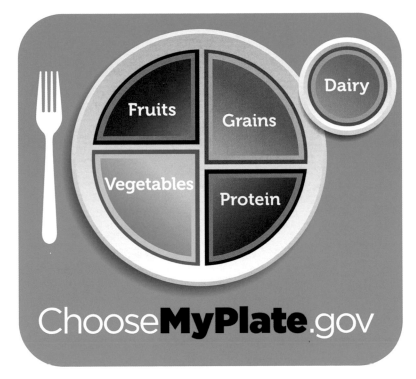

MyPlate allows people to see the recommended amount of each type of food to eat.

Private and nonprofit groups have also launched education
campaigns that stress the importance of healthy eating and nutrition. Former First Lady Michelle Obama launched a fitness
initiative in 2010 called Let's Move! to help combat childhood
obesity and raise healthier kids. Her goal was to teach kids about
exercise and an active lifestyle and to encourage them to keep
healthy habits from childhood into adulthood.

However, the funding for public education campaigns such as MyPlate and Let's Move! are no match for the resources of fast food chains and snack and soda companies. At its height, the 5 A Day fruit and vegetable campaign, sponsored by the National Cancer Institute, had an annual budget of $2 million for promotion, compared to a $3 billion U.S. advertising budget for Coca-Cola and Pepsi combined. With limited money and resources, public education campaigns are unlikely to reach many of the U.S. residents at highest risk for obesity, including poor and minority Americans, recent immigrants, teenagers, and children.

The programs that do succeed in reaching these groups tend to be hands-on and community based. They do not simply tell people to eat right and exercise; they provide practical support and training to help them make healthier lifestyle choices. The Let's Move! program is one example. According to *Governing* magazine, between 2012 and 2016, the city of McAllen, Texas—which had been ranked the most obese city in the United States—reduced its obesity rate by 33 percent after signing on for Obama's program. Although the program has shown positive results, it is unclear whether future presidential administrations will continue funding it. The leaders of several cities have stated that if the federal government will no longer provide money for the initiative, the cities will do it themselves and will try to get private organizations to donate money as well. Many people understand that it is unrealistic to ask most individuals to make heroic efforts to change their own lifestyles as long as the culture they live and work in remains unchanged.

Apathy Versus Action

Efforts to change the nation's food culture are often met with public indifference. Unhealthy eating has become so ingrained that many people believe it is pointless to resist. Parents who insist on serving only healthy foods at home, for example, are powerless to control what their children eat at school or social events, such as birthday parties. When the family dines out at a restaurant or fast food chain, they seldom object as their children order from among the unhealthy meal choices on the kids' menu. It can also be difficult to choose healthy foods over unhealthy foods because unhealthy foods are what people are used to; they are designed to taste good and leave people craving more. As a result of the public's indifference, politicians have been reluctant to stand up to the food industry or propose bold policy actions to change the existing culture.

In recent years, however, there have been signs that public apathy about weight gain and obesity is beginning to give way to action. At the local level, parents, health experts, elected officials, and students have joined together to ban soda and junk food from school vending machines and cafeterias nationwide. Public and media criticism also has compelled some companies to make changes in the way they do business. In June 2012, Disney announced that all foods and beverages that did not meet children's nutritional standards would be banned from being advertised in any way on the Disney Channel, Disney Junior, Disney XD, Radio Disney, and Disney-owned websites for children 12 and under. Additionally, U.S. theme parks were part of the pledge; they cut sodium levels from children's food and promised to increase the amount of fruits and vegetables available.

TAKING RESPONSIBILITY

"Certain myths help maintain the 'lack of ownership' ... That we can or should have exactly what we crave is one of these. That's simply not practical in the world we live in. The myths gain strength from factors beyond our immediate control—the food industry, to name one. But when we take responsibility for how they affect our own lives, change can begin."—Dr. Terese Weinstein Katz, clinical psychologist and eating disorder specialist

Terese Weinstein Katz, "I Want What I Want: Taking Responsibility and Weight Management," *Psychology Today,* May 31, 2011. www.psychologytoday.com/blog/thin-within/201105/i-want-what-i-want-taking-responsibility-and-weight-management.

Additionally, studies have found that people can convince themselves to choose healthy options if they make positive associations with healthy foods and negative associations with unhealthy foods. Wansink and his team offered a lunch buffet to children at a vacation Bible school and found that the name of the foods on the buffet impacted which ones the children chose: "For instance, when we renamed peas 'power peas,' the number of children taking them nearly doubled."[30] Weight loss efforts are improved if people approach them with a positive attitude and see it as something they want to do rather than something they need to do. "If there is any possibility for major social action and policy change," explained Brownell and Battle Horgen, "scientists cannot force it and health leaders cannot mandate it. The public must demand it."[31]

Promoting Fitness

In addition to improving their eating habits, Americans must also get out of their cars, off of their chairs, and tear themselves away from televisions and cell phone screens to increase their level of physical activity. Study after study shows that even moderate physical activity improves the health of people in every age and weight range. Such activity does not require elaborate exercise equipment or membership in fancy gyms. Just walking at a normal pace up the stairs, around the block, through a park, or on city sidewalks can improve long-term health. Exercise benefits the heart and reduces the risk of disease. It also helps maintain bone health and may relieve the symptoms of anxiety and depression. For those who are overweight or obese, it is associated with fewer doctor's visits and hospitalizations. Despite these clear health benefits, many U.S. residents find that it is as difficult to stay fit as it is to eat nutritious foods and reasonably-sized portions. This is especially true in the case of people living below the poverty line. According to *The Atlantic*:

> *Compared to adults making $75,000 or more [per year], those making less than $20,000 [per year] were 50 percent less likely to exercise, 42 percent less likely to drink a lot of water, and 25 percent less likely to eat less fat and sweets ... [Part of the problem] might be that the stressful lives of poor people make sticking to a diet and exercise plan more difficult. It's hard to exercise when you live in an unsafe neighborhood. Stress leads to emotional eating. You can't plan for gym time when you only know your work schedule three days in advance.*[32]

Additionally, many poor people work more than one job, which means they may be too tired or busy to cook healthy meals and get enough exercise.

Public health messages urging people to get in shape help motivate some people, but they are more successful when accompanied by programs and policies that make staying fit convenient and easy. These do not have to be expensive. Some of the most effective fitness programs motivate residents of the same communities to walk and move together. To address parents' safety concerns about allowing their children to walk to school, the Safe Routes to School program, sponsored in part by the CDC, promotes measures that make it safer for kids to walk or bike to school, including changes in city planning that make walking conditions safer and better enforcement of traffic rules. Even the simplest measures can make a difference. Climbing stairs burns more calories per minute than almost any other physical activity, so researchers have experimented with signs posted at the base of shopping mall and subway stairwells

Some businesses and places of work encourage their employees to take "active breaks" during the day to avoid a sedentary lifestyle.

with messages such as, "Your heart needs exercise; here's your chance." They found that once the signs were up, stair use nearly tripled for both thin and overweight people.

Some employers, looking to save on health costs and increase worker productivity, have also gotten in on the fitness act. They have put into place health and wellness programs that include workplace fitness centers and exercise breaks for employees. For example, Kaiser Permanente Health Care keeps its employees healthy through programs such as Go KP. This program provides healthy recipes, and users can track their own wellness goals and join fitness challenges. There are also free fitness centers at many locations. Additionally, the company has updated its cafeterias to meet Partnership for a Healthier America guidelines; they offer healthy checkout options and are working to eliminate sugar-sweetened beverages in their cafeterias and vending machines. The company also offers more than 50 farmer's markets across its facilities and includes a bike-to-work program.

Efforts like this are still the exception, though. Many company headquarters are located along highways or on busy streets where there is no place to walk. Office buildings are often built with inconvenient, poorly lit stairwells. Employees who walk or bike to work may not have a place to wash up or change their clothes. Programs such as Kaiser Permanente's are a positive first step, but Brownell and Battle Horgen said broader change is necessary: "Times, places, and incentives for people to be physically active must be engineered into daily life."[33]

Walker-Friendly Cities

Such changes will be challenging to make because most American cities and suburbs were not designed for physical activity. They were built with cars, not pedestrians, in mind. In some suburbs, there are no sidewalks, and stores are often inaccessible by foot. Suburban residents may be forced to drive to the nearest shopping mall and walk around indoors to stay in shape. In many low-income communities, residents worry about the safety of their neighborhoods and parks and rarely walk or jog at all. To overcome these obstacles, health advocates say, the nation must be willing to support innovative programs and commit resources and funding to make cities and suburbs more conducive to walking, biking, and other physical activity.

In Rancho Cucamonga, California, some important changes have been made in response to Michelle Obama's Let's Move! program. For instance, "the city changed zoning laws to make it legal to grow a community garden throughout most of the city. It finished a 21-mile trail that accommodates runners, bikers and equestrians [horseback riders]."[34] The city also opened more farmers markets that sell fresh, local food. Other cities may encourage walking and biking by adding sidewalks, crosswalks, streetlights, and bike paths to existing roads or a protective strip of parked cars or trees to shield walkers from heavily trafficked streets. Local officials can install bike racks at libraries, parks, schools and other public buildings and hire crossing guards—or recruit parents or other volunteers—to make sure children can safely walk or bike home from school. They can also pass zoning laws and provide tax incentives to builders who construct residential and commercial spaces within walking distance of public transportation.

DEMANDING A HEALTHY LIFE

"We have the opportunity to demand of our leaders, of our healthcare system, of our communities, and of ourselves that the world become a place in which it is possible to live not just a long life but a healthy one."–Dr. Francine Kaufman, author and professor

Francine Kaufman, *Diabesity: The Obesity-Diabetes Epidemic that Threatens America–and What We Must Do to Stop It.* New York, NY: Bantam, 2005, p. 19.

When new communities are designed, measures such as these can be taken right from the beginning. The architects, urban planners, and health experts who belong to a movement called New Urbanism are working in several regions of the country to create walkable communities in which residential areas are a short distance from shops and commercial centers. They point to studies that show that people who live in densely populated places that have sidewalks and shops within walking distance tend to have lower rates of diabetes, high blood pressure, heart disease, and stroke. The goal of the New Urbanists is to reduce Americans' dependence on their cars and restore a sense of community to people's lives in order to improve their overall health.

Healthy Choices in Schools

Schools are an obvious place to start improving the health and fitness of Americans of all income levels. If children are taught to appreciate the benefits of good nutrition and physical fitness early in their school years, they are likely to carry this with them for the rest of their lives. Health advocates say that there are immediate steps federal and state lawmakers can take to put the nation's public schools at the forefront of a campaign to improve public health. They can ensure that they are serving fruits, vegetables, and whole grains and are following new nutrition guidelines. They can ensure that children have enough time to eat lunch to cut down on snacking between classes. They can make the areas around schools junk food–free zones, where fast food chains are not permitted. To improve physical fitness, they can mandate that children get at least 30 minutes of physical activity during the course of the school day and provide funding for local school districts to repair playgrounds and purchase sporting equipment.

Local school officials can also play an important role in improving children's health by supporting nutrition education programs in which children are taught to read food labels and understand serving sizes and calorie counts. These programs can include media literacy training in which students learn to recognize and resist the marketing tactics that fast food chains and snack and soda companies use to appeal to kids. They can also encourage open discussion of cultural attitudes about body image, dangerous weight-loss fads, and the difficulty of fighting the nation's unhealthy food culture.

Many schools promote more than just healthy eating; they also focus on living a healthy lifestyle through groups such as Fuel Up to Play 60, a program started by the National Football

Teaching kids about exercise and giving them the opportunity to be active during the school day is an important step toward overall health.

League (NFL) to encourage kids to lead healthier lives. They offer funds to buy equipment, and some schools even arrange for a pro football player to visit to talk about the importance of eating healthy and staying active. Programs such as this go above and beyond just following nutrition basics and aim to involve kids in making their own healthy choices.

Other schools are experimenting with nontraditional PE classes in which students are taught to have fun and stay fit for life. Rather than ask everyone in a class to play baseball or kick-ball, gym teachers in these programs offer a variety of activities from which kids can choose. During a single class, for example, some students may be kickboxing or doing yoga, while others do in-line skating or canoeing in the school pool. "You have to give them something fun," said childhood obesity expert Reginald Washington, "something they can be successful at."[35]

Whole Kids Foundation

An organization called the Whole Kids Foundation believes that healthy eating during the school day is an important step to overall health. By supporting schools, it is able to reach hundreds of educators and children at the same time while placing value on healthy food choices in the community. The Whole Kids Foundation offers grants to schools that want to help teachers and students create gardens to grow the food that is used in their school cafeteria lunches. It also supports a program to move schools away from the traditional cafeteria food to offer salad bars with a large variety of options. The members of this organization believe that if students are given more choices, they will be more likely to eat salads that they can create themselves. Its website contains lesson plans, resources, activities, and recipes for schools that are trying to make healthy eating and lifestyles a part of their routine.

A Healthy Balance

Even the most successful school and community efforts to curb obesity have a difficult balance to maintain. They must address the environmental forces that promote poor eating habits and sedentary lifestyles without further stigmatizing overweight and obese Americans or deepening the nation's cultural obsession with body image and thinness. Fitness and nutrition programs that focus too heavily on the dangers of weight gain are likely to make obese people feel singled out or hopeless, especially if these individuals have struggled and failed to lose weight. Schools in some states have begun weighing students and testing their fitness. Some send home fitness report cards that identify a child's weight and BMI. In a culture that already emphasizes beauty and thinness, many parents and educators fear that these measures will only make overweight kids feel more self-conscious and may actually cause them to gain more weight.

The mixed signals that Western culture sends about eating and fitness have already taken a heavy toll on Americans of all ages. "Even as kids are bombarded from infancy with messages to chow down foods that experts tell us are practically guaranteed to make them obese," wrote *Consuming Kids* author Susan Linn, "they—girls especially—are being sold the notion that they are supposed to be impossibly thin."[36] It is no wonder that many Americans endanger their health with fad diets, weight-loss pills, and other harmful diet schemes—or that many young adults develop serious eating disorders, such as anorexia and bulimia.

Western society generally equates being thin with being healthy, but this is not always the case. A person can have a low BMI and still be at risk for developing type 2 diabetes, while at the same time, a person with a higher BMI may not be at risk for any diseases. According to the *Huffington Post*, "lean people may lack visible body fat under the skin because it is being stored deeper inside the body, around the organs and in the muscles."[37] In other words, someone who looks thin may still be at risk for diseases that typically affect people who are overweight or obese. Experts say the emphasis should not be on weight, but on health; everyone should try to eat a healthy diet and exercise frequently, regardless of whether or not they think they need to lose weight.

Introduction: A Problem on the Rise

1. Radley Balko, "Living Large: We've Been Misled about the Real Threat Posed by the 'Obesity Crisis'," Cato Institute, November 10, 2005. www.cato.org/pub_display.php?pub_id=5185.

2. Francine R. Kaufman, *Diabesity: The Obesity-Diabetes Epidemic that Threatens America—and What We Must Do to Stop It*. New York, NY: Bantam, 2005, p. 16.

Chapter 1: Americans' Weight and Health

3. "TIME Magazine and ABC News Announce Summit on Obesity," *TIME*, April 12, 2004. content.time.com/time/press_releases/article/0,8599,610179,00.html?iid=tsmodule.

4. Eric Schlosser, *Fast Food Nation: The Dark Side of the All-American Meal*. New York, NY: HarperCollins, 2002, p. 240.

5. "Obesity Rates & Trends Overview," The State of Obesity. stateofobesity.org/obesity-rates-trends-overview/.

6. "Obesity Rates & Trends Overview," The State of Obesity.

7. Kelly D. Brownell and Katherine Battle Horgen, *Food Fight: The Inside Story of the Food Industry, America's Obesity Crisis, & What We Can Do About It*. Chicago, IL: McGraw-Hill Contemporary Books, 2004, p. 6.

8. Paul Campos, *The Obesity Myth: Why America's Obsession with Weight Is Hazardous to Your Health*. New York, NY: Gotham, 2004, p. xv.

9. Rick Berman, "Industry Salivates Over New Cash Cow," *Atlanta Journal-Constitution*, February 23, 2005. www.consumerfreedom.com/oped_detail.cfm/oped/316.

Chapter 2: What Causes American Obesity?

10. Marion Nestle, *Food Politics: How the Food Industry Influences Nutrition and Health.* Berkeley, CA: University of California Press, 2002, p. 16.

11. Quoted in Ellen Ruppel Shell, *The Hungry Gene: The Science of Fat and the Future of Thin.* New York, NY: Atlantic Monthly, 2002, p. 207.

12. Brian Wansink, *Mindless Eating: Why We Eat More Than We Think.* New York, NY: Bantam Books, 2006, e-book.

13. Wansink, *Mindless Eating.*

14. Julia Belluz and Christopher Haubursin, "The Science Is In: Exercise Won't Help You Lose Much Weight," Vox, June 29, 2016. www.vox.com/2016/6/29/12051520/exercise-weight-loss-myth-burn-calories-video.

15. Brownell and Battle Horgen, *Food Fight*, p. 23.

16. Michael Fumento, *The Fat of the Land: The Obesity Epidemic and How Overweight Americans Can Help Themselves.* New York, NY: Viking, 1997, p. 99.

Chapter 3: Children's and Teenagers' Eating Habits and Lifestyle

17. Brownell and Battle Horgen, *Food Fight*, p. 50.

18. "Sugary Drinks and Obesity Fact Sheet," Harvard T. H. Chan School of Public Health, 2017. www.hsph.harvard.edu/nutritionsource/sugary-drinks-fact-sheet/.

19. Schlosser, *Fast Food Nation*, p. 43.

20. Susan Linn, *Consuming Kids: The Hostile Takeover of Childhood.* New York, NY: The New Press, 2004, p. 100.

21. Kaufman, *Diabesity*, p. 220.

22. Quoted in Michael D. Lemonick, "America's Youth Are in Worse Shape Than Ever, But There's a Movement Afoot to Remedy That," *TIME*, June 6, 2005, p. 57.

Chapter 4: The Food Industry's Role in Obesity

23. Quoted in "Sugar: Last Week Tonight with John Oliver

(HBO)," YouTube video, 11:34, posted by LastWeekTonight, October 26, 2014. www.youtube.com/watch?v=MepXBJjsNxs.

24. Quoted in Nestle, *Food Politics*, p. 259.

25. Dan Charles, "An 'Added Sugar' Label Is on the Way for Packaged Food," NPR, May 20, 2016. www.npr.org/sections/the-salt/2016/05/20/478837157/the-added-sugar-label-is-coming-to-a-packaged-food-near-you.

26. Quoted in Brownell and Battle Horgen, *Food Fight*, p. 266.

27. Quoted in Erin Madigan, "'Cheeseburger' Bills Fill State Law-makers' Plates," *Insurance Journal*, March 7, 2005. www.insurance   journal.com/magazines/west/2005/03/07/features/52953.htm.

28. Brownell and Battle Horgen, *Food Fight*, p. 296.

Chapter 5: Healthy Lifestyle Changes

29. Quoted in Geoffrey Cowley and Karen Springen, "A 'Culture of Health': Arkansas Gov. Mike Huckabee Has Put His State on a Fitness Regimen. Can He Do the Same for America?," *TIME*, October 3, 2005, p. 67.

30. Wansink, *Mindless Eating*.

31. Brownell and Battle Horgen, *Food Fight*, p. 286.

32. Olga Khazan, "Rich People Exercise, Poor People Take Diet Pills," *The Atlantic*, August 21, 2014. www.theatlantic.com/health/archive/2014/08/rich-people-exercise-poor-people-take-diet-pills/378852/.

33. Brownell and Battle Horgen, *Food Fight*, p. 96.

34. Mattie Quinn, "Without Michelle Obama, What Will Happen to 'Let's Move'?," *Governing*, December 15, 2016. www.governing.com/topics/health-human-services/gov-obesity-michelle-obama.html.

35. Quoted in Lemonick, "America's Youth Are in Worse Shape Than Ever," p. 57.

36. Linn, *Consuming Kids*, p. 102.

37. Oz Garcia, "Being Thin Isn't the Same as Being Healthy," *Huffington Post*, October 8, 2011. www.huffingtonpost.com/oz-garcia/thin-health_b_918942.html.

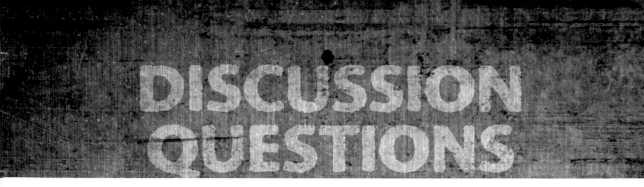

Chapter 1: Americans' Weight and Health

1. Why do race and economics make such a difference in obesity rates?

2. What are the environmental factors that health experts suggest make residents of poor communities more susceptible to being overweight or obese?

3. Why is it difficult to determine how many deaths are caused by excessive weight gain and obesity?

Chapter 2: What Causes American Obesity?

1. Why do people continue to eat fast food if they know it is so bad for their health?

2. What reasons does the author cite for Americans' lack of physical activity?

3. Why do many health experts conclude that environmental and not biological or genetic factors are the main causes of the obesity epidemic?

Chapter 3: Children's and Teenagers' Eating Habits and Lifestyle

1. What changes have occurred in children's diets in the past several decades that help explain the rising rate of childhood obesity?

2. Why are fast food chains and other food companies so successful at getting Americans to buy their products?

3. What are the lifestyle factors that make the current generation of American children the least active generation in history?

Chapter 4: The Food Industry's Role in Obesity

1. How is the nation's public health campaign against cigarette smoking similar to or different from efforts to reform the food industry?

2. What can Americans do to avoid "falling prey" to the food industry's advertising campaigns?

3. How does the food industry defend itself against charges that it has contributed to the obesity epidemic?

Chapter 5: Healthy Lifestyle Changes

1. Why do many health advocates believe a drug or medical treatment for obesity is unlikely to be effective on a large scale?

2. What does it mean to engineer physical activity into daily life?

3. Why are Americans so hesitant to make a change in their diet and lifestyle?

American Diabetes Association (ADA)
2451 Crystal Drive, Suite 900
Arlington, VA 22202
1-800-342-2383
www.diabetes.org/home.jsp
The ADA provides diabetes research, education, and advocacy on behalf of people living with the disease.

The American Obesity Association
1110 Bonifant Street
Suite 500
Silver Spring, MD 20910
(301) 563-6526
www.obesity.org
The American Obesity Association is an education and advocacy group that fights discrimination against Americans who are obese and lobbies government and health groups to treat obesity as a disease rather than a matter of personal failure.

The Center for Consumer Freedom (CCF)
P.O. Box 34557
Washington, D.C. 20043
(202) 463-7112
www.consumerfreedom.com
The CCF is a coalition of restaurants and food companies that works to promote free-market principles and consumer choice. CCF lobbies against measures such as restrictions on food marketing and snack food taxes.

Center for Science in the Public Interest (CSPI)
1220 L St. N.W.
Suite 300
Washington, D.C. 20005
(202) 332-9110
www.cspinet.org
A strong voice in the movement to reform the food industry, CSPI conducts scientific research on nutrition issues and lobbies for measures such as food marketing restrictions and snack taxes. The group also takes an active role in lawsuits against food and soda companies.

The Edible Schoolyard
1517 Shattuck Avenue
Berkeley, CA 94709
(510) 843-3811
www.edibleschoolyard.org
Founded by renowned chef Alice Waters of Berkeley, California, the Edible Schoolyard provides urban public school students with an organic garden and teaches them to grow, harvest, and prepare fresh produce. The project has become a model for school garden and nutrition projects around the country.

The President's Fitness Challenge
1101 Wootton Parkway
Suite 560
Rockville, MD 20852
(240) 276-9567
www.presidentschallenge.org
Sponsored by the President's Council on Physical Fitness, Sports and Nutrition, which is a group of fitness advisers to the U.S. president, this program encourages Americans of all ages to become more physically active.

Books

Dickmann, Nancy. *What You Need to Know about Obesity*. North Mankato, MN: Capstone Press, 2016.
The causes of and possible solutions to obesity are presented alongside real-life stories from kids who have dealt with obesity in their own lives.

Ford, Jean. *No Quick Fix: Fad Diets & Weight-Loss Miracles*. Broomall, PA: Mason Crest, 2015.
There are many diets and pills out there that promise fast, easy weight loss with little to no effort. Unfortunately, they either do not work or work too well, with unhealthy consequences for the body. This book discusses the traps the diet industry sets up and how to avoid them.

Perdew, Laura. *Asking Questions about Food Advertising*. Ann Arbor, MI: Cherry Lake Publishing, 2016.
Advertisers use many tricks to get people to buy their products. Being aware of these tricks is one way people can avoid buying and eating too much food.

Ventura, Marne. *Nutrition Myths, Busted!*. North Mankato, MN: 12-Story Library, 2017.
Misinformation about nutrition is spread around by the media as well as by people who hear a story and assume it is true. This book discusses 12 of the biggest myths about nutrition and exposes the truth about each one.

Wansink, Brian. *Mindless Eating: Why We Eat More Than We Think*. New York, NY: Bantam Books, 2006.
Through a series of studies, Wansink and his team of graduate students show that people eat for more reasons than just hunger, including boredom, distraction, and emotional satisfaction. When people are aware of the reasons why they are eating, they can make a more conscious effort to eat less as well as to eat healthier foods.

Websites

Don't Buy It! Project

www.pbskids.org/dontbuyit

Part of the *Don't Buy It!* project sponsored by the Public Broadcasting Service (PBS), this website is intended to help young people become media-savvy consumers. An area of the website called "Food Advertising Tricks" explores the tactics food companies use to entice people to buy their products.

KidsHealth

www.kidshealth.org

The kids' and teens' pages of this website feature physician-reviewed articles, animations, games, a BMI calculator, and resources on health and nutrition issues. KidsHealth is sponsored by the Nemours Foundation's Center for Children's Health Media, which works to provide up-to-date information on children's health issues.

National Center for Health Statistics of the Centers for Disease Control and Prevention

www.cdc.gov/nchs/

The CDC's National Center for Health Statistics offers the latest data from national health and nutrition surveys on weight gain and obesity.

Take Charge of Your Health: A Guide for Teenagers

www.win.niddk.nih.gov/publications/take_charge.htm

This website is a guide to healthy living for teenagers sponsored by the Weight Control Information Network (WIN). WIN is a service of government health groups, including the National Institutes of Health. This website includes features on diet, portion size, and exercise that encourage teens to take charge of their own health.

The U.S. Department of Agriculture's Choose My Plate

www.choosemyplate.gov/

This website showcases the USDA's updated dietary guidelines. An interactive feature allows users to plug in their age and activity levels and choose the foods and daily calorie counts that are right for them.

INDEX